KU-796-663

IRISH BIRDS

WITHDRAWN FROM STOCK

For Louise Cabot, with love and admiration

IRISH BIRDS

DAVID CABOT

The author would like to thank Myles Archibald,
Helen Brocklehurst and Isobel Smales of HarperCollins for
encouragement and assistance during the preparation of
this guide. He would also like to thank Véronique Alexandre
for valued editorial assistance.

HarperCollins*Publishers* Ltd.
77-85 Fulham Palace Road
London
W6 8JB

The Collins website address is:
www.collins.co.uk

Collins is a registered trademark of
HarperCollins*Publishers* Ltd.

First published in 1995
This revised edition published 2004

Text © 2004 David Cabot
Artwork and maps © 1987 HarperCollins Publishers
Photographs © 1995 David Cabot, unless otherwise stated

10 09 08 07 06 05 04
10 9 8 7 6 5 4 3 2 1
The author asserts his moral right to be identified as the author
of this work. All rights reserved.

All rights reserved. No parts of this publication may be reproduced,
stored in a retrieval system or transmitted, in any form or by any
means, electronic, mechanical, photocopying, recording or otherwise,
without the prior permission of the publishers.

A catalogue record for this book is available from the
British Library.

ISBN 0 00 717610 4
Illustrations by Norman Arlott
Printed and bound in Hong Kong by Printing Express

CONTENTS

ABOUT THIS BOOK

This book has been specially designed for those with a general interest in Irish birds who would like a simple, easy-to-use and well-illustrated guide to the most frequently occurring birds in Ireland. Rare and unusual species have been deliberately left out as these are for the more experienced birdwatcher and several other books already cater for these interests. However, a few scarce birds, such as the Roseate Tern, have been included when they are of particular Irish significance. So, 167 birds have been carefully selected for this guide on the basis that they are the most likely to be encountered by the beginner and the non-specialist birdwatcher.

There are many different ways of presenting a guide to birds. The system adopted here is intended to be helpful and practical to the observer: birds are grouped together according to the major habitat types in which they are most likely to be seen. So, if you are walking in a woodland, strolling along the seashore, or watching birds in your garden, you can check on what you have seen by quickly flicking through the relevant habitat sections. However, most classification systems have their failings and the one offered here is not without defects. Birds are highly mobile and likely to cross habitat boundaries, thus making allocation to a particular section a difficult affair. For instance, one of our commonest birds, the blackbird, is widely scattered throughout farmland habitats and is also a woodland inhabitant. In this guide, however, it is to be found in the 'Gardens, Parks and Buildings' section, since most people will encounter blackbirds in their gardens. So, while trying to achieve the impossible, I have had to exercise judgement and make choices.

While giving what I believe are the essential identification characteristics for each of the 167 species (along with notes on their distribution), I have also added extra information on numbers and migrations. In order to present the most up-to-date information, I have relied on several basic texts, which are mentioned in 'What Next?' on p.236. The maps for each species are intended as a rough guide to their distribution. Yellow indicates that the bird is only a summer visitor, blue indicates that the bird is only a winter visitor, and green indicates that the bird is resident and therefore can be seen all year round.

Irish bird names have been taken from BirdWatch Ireland's *Checklist of Birds of Ireland* (1999); the numbers of most breeding birds have been taken from *The*

New Atlas of Breeding Birds (1993); numbers of breeding seabirds from *Seabird 2000* surveys, conducted mainly during 1999–2002, under the principal sponsorship of the British Joint Nature Conservation Committee, BirdWatch Ireland, the Seabird Group and National Parks & Wildlife, Dublin, and published in *Seabird Populations of Britain and Ireland* (2004); most wildfowl data from the *Atlas of Anatidae Populations* (1996); the size of birds – total length of dead bird on its back, from the tip of the bill to the tip of the tail – from *The Handbook of the Birds of Europe and the Middle East and North America* (1977–1994). For further details see pages 236–237.

The following are thanked for their help and assistance: Oran O'Sullivan (selection of additional species); Dr. Steve Newton, Tim Dunn and Dr. Ian Mitchell (seabird data), Alex Copland (corncrake data) and Oscar Merne (barnacle goose census data).

David Cabot
November 2003

GENERAL NOTES ON BIRD IDENTIFICATION

Many beginners feel intimidated by the apparent difficulties of identifying so many different kinds of birds. The biggest problem is getting close enough to a bird to see it properly. There are two ways of overcoming this. Set up a simple bird table in your garden, close to a window, where you can watch many different birds coming and going. This is how I started off when, at an early age, I became curious about birds. The other way is to visit wildfowl or other bird collections where birds are tame and allow close approach. A few good places to start off from will be St. Stephen's Green, Dublin; The Lough, Cork; Dublin Zoo, Phoenix Park; The North Slob Wildfowl Reserve, Co. Wexford; Castle Espie Wildfowl Collection; Comber, Co. Down; and Fota Wildlife Park, Co. Cork. After you have acquired the basic rudiments of bird identification, the next – and most enjoyable – way to increase your knowledge is to join a field outing of a bird club or organisation, or better still, tag along with a friend who is more experienced than you. It is amazing how quickly you will learn to identify not only by plumage but also by the songs and the way birds move or fly, a greater number of birds. The only piece of equipment needed is a pair of reasonably priced binoculars (magnification of 8x30 is best to start with), plus a notebook to record what you see.

There are seven basic categories of information that will aid you on your path to successful bird identification:

(1) SIZE: Is it larger or smaller than, or the same size as, a bird familiar to you (such as the robin or the blackbird)?

(2) SHAPE: What kind of shape is the body (round, plump, thin); head (big, small); neck (long, short, bent); bill (long, short, thick, thin, upturned, or downturned); wings (long, short, pointed, rounded, forming fingers); legs (long, short); tail (long, short, forked, square, rounded), and so on?

(3) BEHAVIOUR: How does it move? Does it bob or wag its tail? Does it do anything unusual? How does it feed? How does it behave in water (sitting, diving, taking off, landing)? Does it wade? Does it dive into the water from the sky? Does it run along the tideline?

(4) FLIGHT: Does it fly slow or fast, high or low; what about the wingbeats? Does it soar in lines in a "V" formation? Does it fly in a straight line, or in undulations?

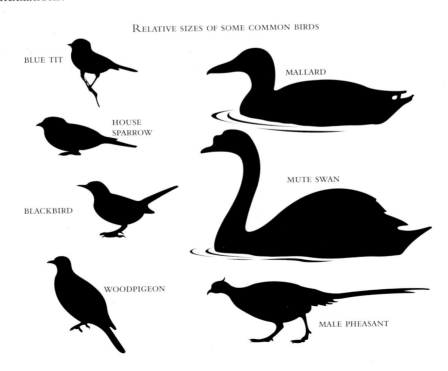

RELATIVE SIZES OF SOME COMMON BIRDS

BLUE TIT

MALLARD

HOUSE SPARROW

MUTE SWAN

BLACKBIRD

WOODPIGEON

MALE PHEASANT

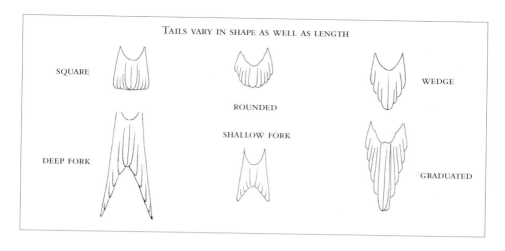

(5) PLUMAGE MARKS: Are there any distinguishing plumage details? Does it have a head stripe above, through, or below the eye? Are there any significant colours, streaking, or spotting? What colour are the rump and tail feathers? Are there any wing bars or patterns on the upper sides of the wings?

(6) CALL AND SONG: What kind of call note does it make for a normal contact or flight call, and when it is disturbed or threatened? How does the song sound? Does the bird sing on the wing, from a perch, or at night?

(7) HABITAT: In what kind of environment does it occur, and at what time of the year?

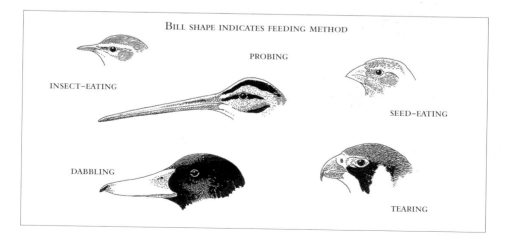

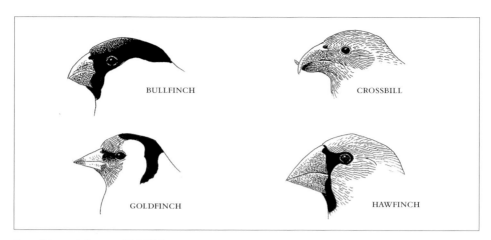

Even within a particular group of birds bill shapes may vary:
Finches – the harder the food, the heavier and stronger the bill
Ducks – bills are adapted to cope with the main food taken (see pp. 116-7)

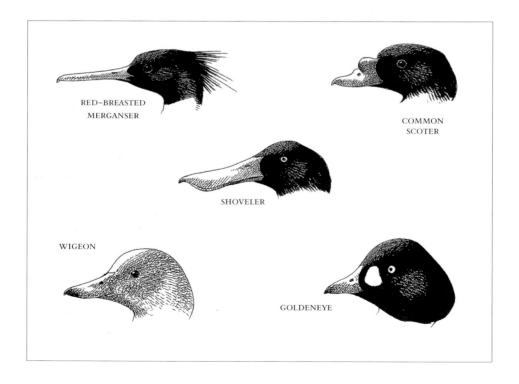

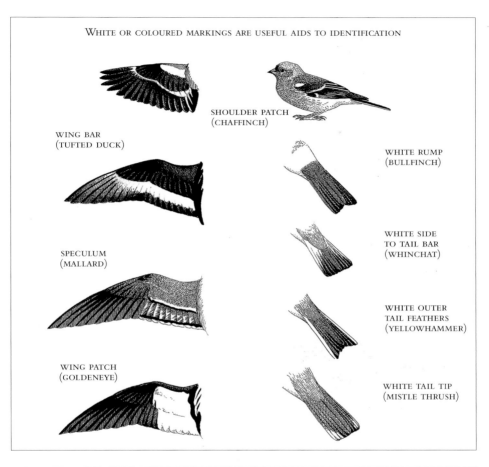

WHITE OR COLOURED MARKINGS ARE USEFUL AIDS TO IDENTIFICATION

WING BAR
(TUFTED DUCK)

SHOULDER PATCH
(CHAFFINCH)

WHITE RUMP
(BULLFINCH)

SPECULUM
(MALLARD)

WHITE SIDE
TO TAIL BAR
(WHINCHAT)

WING PATCH
(GOLDENEYE)

WHITE OUTER
TAIL FEATHERS
(YELLOWHAMMER)

WHITE TAIL TIP
(MISTLE THRUSH)

HEAD PATTERNS CAN ALSO HELP WITH IDENTIFICATION

CREST (JAY)

EYESTRIPE
(WILLOW WARBLER)

BIB (GREY WAGTAIL)

MOUSTACHE
(FEMALE REED BUNTING)

Gardens, Parks and Buildings

Gardens at Muckross House, Killarney National Park, Co. Kerry. The diverse tree and shrub layers provide a wide range of breeding habitats for most garden birds.

Most people first come in close contact with birds in their gardens or in parks. Garden habitats usually have good nesting sites in hedges, bushes and trees, as well as a good supply of foods, owing mostly to the gardening activities. If extra food is offered on a bird table, the population of visiting birds increases dramatically.

A garden ideal for birds will have uncultivated parts that will appeal to seed-eating finches; it will have a small pond or area of water where the birds can bathe, preen and drink; there will be attractive berried shrubs like cotoneaster for the thrushes, plenty of nesting cover in thick hedges, shrubs and small trees; and a bird table placed out of reach of cats and well-stocked with peanuts, fat and other scraps (remember that white bread is not nutritious enough).

Bird tables allow close-up views of a wide variety of birds. In a recent survey (winter 2001–2002) - organised by BirdWatch Ireland - covering more than 900 suburban and urban garden bird tables, the top 10 birds recorded were: robin, blackbird, blue tit, chaffinch, magpie, greenfinch, great tit, wren, song thrush and house sparrow. Following close behind were: coal tit, dunnock, starling, jackdaw and rook. Less frequent visitors would be the fieldfare and the redwing, in hard weather, along with the collared dove, pied wagtail and blackcap.

Manicured parkland, Phoenix Park, Dublin. Despite its tidy appearance the park is a favourite location for blackbirds, thrushes, robins, tits, chaffinches, magpies, sparrowhawks and many other species. (Photo: Redmond Cabot)

Also to be found in gardens and parks are bullfinches, long-tailed tits and goldcrests, all looking for food during the winter. Similarly, sparrowhawks find it profitable to swoop through gardens and parks to catch and kill unsuspecting birds.

As for buildings and man-made structures, they play an essential role in offering nesting sites to the swift, house martin and, to a lesser extent, to starlings, house sparrows and jackdaws, all of which are features of the urban environment and provide you with daily opportunities - on the street, on a train, or on a bus - to sharpen up your observation skills.

Jackdaw

Corvus monedula

Cág

COMMON RESIDENT

33–34 CM

ADULT

The jackdaw, the smallest and most compact of the black crows, has a silvery, ash-grey nape and sides to the head which contrast with the black crown, back and wings, while the underparts are a darker grey. The eye is noticeably pale grey in adults. The shorter bill, the jerky, rapid flight, as well as the characteristic "tchak" call distinguish it from the rook (p.47) and other crows. It is very aerobatic, turning, twisting and swerving, especially in flocks. On the ground it has a perky gait, moving rapidly while feeding mainly on insects and seeds. Jackdaws are very gregarious, forming large flocks – often with rooks – in the winter and autumn, when they roost in trees, woods, or on buildings. While common in the urban environment, where unused chimney pots are favoured nesting sites, they are also found throughout the countryside. They nest in holes in trees, sometimes in rabbit burrows, recesses in ruined buildings and in cliffs. They are found on many of the islands. Numbers in Ireland have increased greatly since the 1950s; the jackdaw is commoner here than in equivalent habitats in Britain. There are about 210,000 pairs in Ireland, found in almost all areas. Some British jackdaws migrate to Ireland during winter.

ADULT

Magpie

Pica pica
Snag breac
VERY COMMON RESIDENT
44–46 CM

The magpie is unmistakable
with its contrasting black-
and-white plumage and a
long, wedge-shaped tail. Its
behaviour is extrovert, involving
a great deal of noise and activity. Irish
magpies are reputedly descended from one flock, which arrived
in Wexford in 1676. Now widespread throughout the country and
even on the islands and exposed cliffs, their population has increased
dramatically since 1960. There are now about 320,000 breeding pairs. First
recorded in Dublin in 1852, their numbers there have almost reached pest
proportions, with some of the highest urban densities (16 pairs/km^2)
recorded in Ireland and Britain. There are noisy nuptial gatherings in spring
and, once paired, they tend to be monogamous. Despite their long
chattering "cack-cack-cack" call, they can sometimes be heard singing a
subtle song consisting of babbling notes interspersed with whistling and
piping sounds. They are well known for their impish tormenting of cats
and dogs, as well as for their predilection for the eggs of young songbirds.
They are non-migratory, remaining generally within 1km of their natal
area. Communal roosts attract up to 100 birds in the autumn.

ADULT

ADULT

Collared Dove

Streptopelia decaocto

Fearán baicdhubh

RECENT COLONIST, WIDESPREAD RESIDENT

31—33 CM

This tame dove takes its name from the narrow, black half collar at the back of its head. It looks like a small grey pigeon, with white tips to the outer tail feathers. Its persistent calls resonate as "ku-kroo-ku". Its flight is fast and it frequently perches on telephone wires, TV aerials and rooftops. It is our only small resident dove. Like the magpie (p.16), it is an invader, but with a more recent and dramatic entry. Formerly restricted to Turkey and the Balkans, a population explosion took the bird on a north-westwardly errand across Europe to England (1955), Scotland (1957) and Ireland (1959). Since then it has spread throughout the country, and is commonest in urban areas, though also found frequenting the open countryside around farms, where this cereal eater finds appropriate food. There are about 30,000 breeding pairs. Its colonisation is attributed to exploitation of an empty ecological niche bereft of any competition, and also to prolific breeding activities. Four to six broods are raised each year over a protracted breeding season, with the female often attending to the fledged young while "off duty" from incubating the next clutch. Large flocks have been recorded, particularly in eastern Ireland, but numbers appear to have decreased in recent years.

ADULT

ADULT

Starling

Sturnus vulgaris
Druid
VERY COMMON RESIDENT
37–42 CM

Starlings are quarrelsome, thrustful and noisy birds, frequently calling their harsh "tcheer". Plump in form, with a short tail, pointed wings and a long, sharp bill, the adults have an iridescent purple-green-blue-black plumage, which has a spangled appearance in winter. The juveniles are mouse-brown, with a whitish brown throat. Starlings are opportunists, equally at home in urban and rural environments. They nest in roofs, walls and tree holes, and are catholic feeders at bird tables, refuse dumps and on open pasture, where they often follow cattle or sheep in the hope of catching insects being disturbed. On the ground they are a bustle of activity with their quick, jerky movements, darting their bills into the soil to grab insect larvae. Although now ubiquitous throughout Ireland - with about 360,000 breeding pairs, they became nearly extinct due to climatic amelioration in the early 19th century. The coordinated movements of large wheeling flocks prior to roosting in the autumn make for one of the most spectacular sights of bird life. They will go out and feed 20-30km from their established roosts. During autumn there is a large influx of birds from Scandinavia, Holland, Poland, north Britain and north Germany.

JUVENILE

ADULT SUMMER

ADULT WINTER

Blackbird

Turdus merula

Lon dubh

VERY COMMON RESIDENT

24–25 CM

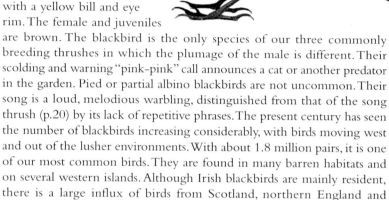

JUVENILE

The blackbird is one of our most familiar garden birds and the principal songster of the dawn chorus. The male is jet black, with a yellow bill and eye rim. The female and juveniles are brown. The blackbird is the only species of our three commonly breeding thrushes in which the plumage of the male is different. Their scolding and warning "pink-pink" call announces a cat or another predator in the garden. Pied or partial albino blackbirds are not uncommon. Their song is a loud, melodious warbling, distinguished from that of the song thrush (p.20) by its lack of repetitive phrases. The present century has seen the number of blackbirds increasing considerably, with birds moving west and out of the lusher environments. With about 1.8 million pairs, it is one of our most common birds. They are found in many barren habitats and on several western islands. Although Irish blackbirds are mainly resident, there is a large influx of birds from Scotland, northern England and Scandinavia during October and November. These autumn/winter immigrants often occur in small flocks or mixed with other thrushes.

See 'Thrushes' p.56

ADULT MALE

Song Thrush

Turdus philomelos
Smólach ceoil
VERY COMMON RESIDENT
23 CM

The song thrush is brown-backed with a spotted chest, and is distinguished from its cousins, the fieldfare (p.57) and redwing (p.58), by its smaller size and uniform upper parts as well as the warmer buff of its breast, marked with a few spots. The song thrush is as widely distributed throughout Ireland as the blackbird, but it is less numerous with only about 390,000 pairs. It is also less conspicuous, and a more skulking feeder. When on the ground, it runs short distances, stops and cocks its head looking for food on the surface. Earthworms and slugs are snapped up, while snails are taken to a rock anvil for smashing them apart. The song is a remarkable feature – loud, clear and vigorous, consisting of a succession of simple phrases, many repeated two or three times. Under ordinary conditions the song will carry for 400m. While sensitive to severe weather conditions - with high mortality rates, there have been no long-term changes in the numbers of song thrushes in Ireland. Many Scottish- and northern English-bred birds migrate to Ireland in October/November. As far as is known, the Irish song thrush is non-migratory, although there are conflicting statements about this in the literature.

See 'Thrushes' p.56

ADULT

SPARROWS & BUNTINGS

House sparrow (p.22) and tree sparrow (p.183), yellowhammer (p.61) and reed bunting (p.141), snow bunting (p.207) and Lapland
bunting (p.207)

- roughly house sparrow-sized, with a similar stocky shape
- short, almost conical, seed-eating bills
- longish, squared tails
- sexes differ in all species included here, except the tree sparrow
- few, apart from the snow bunting, have wing bars or patches

FINCHES

Chaffinch (p.23), greenfinch (p.24), bullfinch (p.25), goldfinch (p.60), siskin (p.85), redpoll (p.86), crossbill (p.87), linnet (p.103) and twite (p.184)

- vary in size from being slightly smaller than a sparrow, to slightly larger
- strong bills adapted for dealing with seeds of varying size, hardness and accessibility
- shallowly forked tails
- sexes differ in some species, are alike in others
- the position and colour of wing and tail markings, best seen in flight, help in identification:
    white wing bar or patch – chaffinch and snow bunting
    white rump – bullfinch and goldfinch
    white sides to tail – chaffinch and linnet
    yellow wing bar or patch – greenfinch, goldfinch and siskin
    yellow sides to tail – greenfinch and siskin
- young birds of the following species are streaky, greenish, or brownish, and can be difficult to identify: greenfinch, goldfinch, siskin, linnet and redpoll. (See also juvenile yellowhammer and reed bunting.) Habitat is often a useful clue to the likely species.

House Sparrow

Passer domesticus
Gealbhan binne
VERY COMMON RESIDENT
DECLINING
14–15 CM

The house sparrow is one of our most familiar birds, closely associated with man, and confined to cultivated land and to the vicinity of human habitation.

ADULT FEMALE

Males have a dark-grey crown, chestnut nape, black throat and whitish cheeks. The hen is brown, with a streaked back. Found widespread across the country, with about one million pairs, it is now declining. They probably arrived in Ireland with the first Neolithic farmers, about 6,000 years ago. Sparrows are busy, bustling and rather aggressive social birds, nesting colonially and feeding, bathing and loafing together. They will displace swallows and house martins to take over their nests, and will colonise nest boxes unless the entrance diameter is less than 2.8 cm. They are basically seed eaters, thus turning into agricultural pests in some areas. There are curious "sparrow party" courtships in spring when several males hop around a hen with loud chirpings, drooped wings and elated tails and heads. There is also "rough and tumble" behaviour amongst males, with the hen often joining in. Essentially sedentary, some movement of birds occurs in spring and autumn.

See 'Sparrows' p.21

ADULT MALE SUMMER

Chaffinch

Fringilla coelebs

Rí rua

VERY COMMON RESIDENT

PASSAGE MIGRANT AND WINTER VISITOR (SEPT–APRIL)

14.5 CM

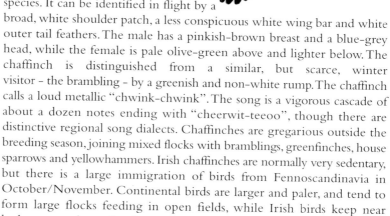

ADULT
FEMALE

One of our commonest birds with just over two million breeding pairs, it occurs wherever trees and bushes are present. The highest densities are found in broad-leaved woodlands. In Kerry oakwoods it was found to be the most abundant species. It can be identified in flight by a broad, white shoulder patch, a less conspicuous white wing bar and white outer tail feathers. The male has a pinkish-brown breast and a blue-grey head, while the female is pale olive-green above and lighter below. The chaffinch is distinguished from a similar, but scarce, winter visitor - the brambling - by a greenish and non-white rump. The chaffinch calls a loud metallic "chwink-chwink". The song is a vigorous cascade of about a dozen notes ending with "cheerwit-teeoo", though there are distinctive regional song dialects. Chaffinches are gregarious outside the breeding season, joining mixed flocks with bramblings, greenfinches, house sparrows and yellowhammers. Irish chaffinches are normally very sedentary, but there is a large immigration of birds from Fennoscandinavia in October/November. Continental birds are larger and paler, and tend to form large flocks feeding in open fields, while Irish birds keep near hedgerows and woodlands.

See 'Finches' p.21

ADULT MALE
SUMMER

Greenfinch

Carduelis chloris
Glasán darach
COMMON RESIDENT
PASSAGE MIGRANT AND WINTER VISITOR (SEPT–MAY)
15 CM

ADULT FEMALE

The greenfinch has a bulky body and a stout
bill. Males are olive-green, with a brighter
yellow-green rump and bright yellow patches
on the primary wing feathers and sides to the tail.
Females are duller and greyer, and less yellow, whereas young birds
are brown and heavily streaked. Once relatively more common in the
countryside, the greenfinch has now become very much a suburban bird
and is quite common in gardens and parks, especially in the east or south-
east. A characteristic, long-drawn-out and reiterated "dzee" is sung from
tall trees, while its true song consists of a varied vocabulary, with notes
strung together in a series of repetitive twittering phrases. It is one of the
top six most frequent bird table attenders, with as many as 100 individuals
visiting a single table in good suburban habitat. Most Irish birds are
sedentary, with some tendency for southward movement in winter. There
is an autumn migration into Ireland from Britain; larger numbers are noted
at coastal sites in September and October. A return passage occurs in April
and May. During the winter, greenfinches may form mixed flocks with
other finches. Recently established forestry plantations in western areas
have provided new habitat where the species was once absent. About
160,000 pairs breed in Ireland.

See 'Finches' p.21

ADULT MALE

Bullfinch

Pyrrhula pyrrhula
Corcrán coille
COMMON RESIDENT
14.5 CM–16.5 CM

ADULT FEMALE

The bullfinch is never easy to see because of its secretive habits, preferring to stay in thickets or dense vegetation, and rarely landing on the ground. They are usually glimpsed flitting along hedgerows - singly, in pairs, or in a family party. Chunky in flight, their pure white rumps catch the eye. The male is handsome, with striking, bright rose-red underparts, blue-grey upper parts, a black cap, a black chin and a stubby black bill. The female has pinkish-grey underparts, while juveniles are browner than the female and without the black cap. Their soft and plaintive "deu-deu" call often announces their presence before they appear. They have no proper song. The most solitary of finches, they are widespread throughout Ireland, except in the harsh western extremities of the counties of Donegal, Mayo, Galway and Kerry. There are about 100,000 breeding pairs. Notorious as pests of commercial fruit trees (especially apple, pear, plum and gooseberry), a single bird can knock off up to 45 buds per minute. Most attacks occur between February and April, when their natural food, seeds, is scarcest. Reputedly paired for life, bullfinches are infrequent bird-table visitors.

See 'Finches' p.21

ADULT MALE

Pied/White Wagtail

Motacilla alba

Glasóg shráide

COMMON RESIDENT

18 CM

The pied wagtail is widespread throughout Ireland and occurs in towns, gardens, around farms, and in the open countryside. The contrasting black-and-white plumage and a long tail bobbing rhythmically up and down make for easy identification. In the male, the crown, all upper parts, throat and upper breast are black in summer. The female's back is greyer. Most of the black bib is lost in winter. Pied wagtails have a brisk gait, a swift run and a bobbing tail, and can be seen leaping around, often snatching an insect flying above them. The legs are long and slender, and their call is a lively "tchizzik" - with the alarm note going "tchnik". It is often, but not always, seen by water and frequently feeds amongst cattle that

WHITE WAGTAIL
ADULT SUMMER

disturb insects. During winter, the birds spend 90 per cent of the daytime feeding, chasing and catching a small insect every 3 or 4 seconds, in order to maintain their energy balance. In autumn they often roost communally in reed beds or even green-houses, where they find warmth and protection from predators. Since 1929 there has been a famous roost in the plane trees of O'Connell Street, Dublin, where up to 3,600 wagtails have been counted. Most birds remain in the country all year, though a few migrate southwards in August to October, returning between the end of February and the end of April. About 130,000 pairs breed. The white wagtail – grey back and rump; black bib separated from black head – occurs as a passage migrant during spring and autumn.

PIED WAGTAIL
MALE SUMMER

Robin

Erithacus rubecula
Spideog
VERY COMMON RESIDENT
14 CM

Both sexes are olive-brown above, with a bright orange forehead, throat and breast. Juveniles have no orange tint and are speckled brown. They are common in gardens, woodlands and hedgerow landscape, with about 2 million breeding pairs. The robin's scolding call is a "tic-tic" and the alarm note is a thin "tswee". The normal song is a melodious, somewhat plaintive, warbling. Uncharacteristically for birds, males defend territories throughout the year whereas the females are likely to wander off in winter, though not more than 5 km away from the breeding site. Most of their food – insects, earthworms, beetles – is collected on the ground by darting down from a perch and then returning. Robins are very susceptible to cold weather, especially snow. Adults are highly secretive during the nesting period; the nest is usually near the base of a hedge or earth bank. However, it is not difficult for the cuckoo to find it, and often appropriate it too. Irish robins are mostly sedentary, but a few migrate south. From mid-August to November, there is an influx of continental robins migrating to south-west Europe and north Africa.

JUVENILE

ADULT

Dunnock

Prunella modularis

Donnóg

VERY COMMON RESIDENT

14.5 CM

Once called the hedge sparrow, its thin bill, fit to catch insects, clearly shows it to be no relation to the heavy-billed, seed-eating sparrow family. Dunnock means a "dun-coloured bird", which it certainly is. The dunnock is inconspicuous and rather featureless, and best described as having a rich brown and dark grey plumage. The sexes are similarly coloured, while juveniles are more rufous and spotted. The least spectacular of garden birds, the dunnock feeds on the ground with a shuffling, and almost crawling, gait. Solitary by nature, its song is a short and fast jingle, similar to the wren's, but not so vigorous. Its alarm call is a sharp "tseep". Its dull plumage and shy demeanour hides a rich and complicated social life. Males often hold overlapping territories in which there are dominant and sub-dominant males. Both types may mate with the same female and polygamy (be it polyandry or polygynandry) is widespread among dunnocks. The Irish birds are sedentary and seldom move more than 1 km. Some continental migratory dunnocks may pass through Ireland in the autumn. About 810,000 pairs breed in Ireland.

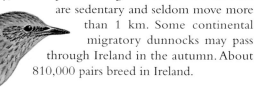

JUVENILE

ADULT

Wren

Troglodytes troglodytes
Dreoilín
VERY COMMON RESIDENT
9–10 CM

The wren is tiny and diminutive in size – only the goldcrest (p.78) is smaller – and is russet-brown with a short, usually cocked, tail. It has a pale eyestripe. The wren is a bustling, busy bird, poking and probing into crevices, holes and vegetation in search of food. Numbering about 3 million breeding pairs, it is a highly adaptable bird with a presence in every habitat, including remote uninhabited islands. It is frequent in shrubby gardens and sheltered bushes, and is very sedentary, with no ringing recoveries exceeding a radius of 9 km from where they were ringed. Its presence is often announced by the alarm call "churr" and

JUVENILE "tik–tik–tik". The male builds several dome-shaped nests and the female selects one, lines it with feathers, and lays 5-6 eggs. There are usually two clutches a year, the male taking the first fledged brood to roost in a spare nest while the female is incubating a second. It was traditionally "hunted" and displayed on a pole on St. Stephen's day (December 26). The origin of this custom is obscure, but probably linked to new year ceremonies of early Neolithic farmers. There is evidence of passage birds in coastal areas in October-November, and again in March-April.

ADULT

TITS

Great (p.31), blue (p.32), coal (p.33) and long-tailed (p.82) tits

• small, plump, agile and active; mostly hole-nesting birds

• short, fairly slim but strong bills, capable of hammering open seeds and nuts

• the sexes are similar, with the young generally less brightly coloured than adults

• woodland birds by nature, but the three commonest species (blue, great and coal) are now regular garden visitors/dwellers, while long-tailed tits also occasionally come to bird tables

JUVENILE GREAT TIT

JUVENILE BLUE TIT

JUVENILE COAL TIT

Great Tit

Parus major

Meantán mór

VERY COMMON RESIDENT

14 CM

ADULT

The great tit is the largest and strongest of the tits, and is a handsome, lively bird. The head and neck are glossy black, the cheeks a brilliant white, and a broad black band extends down the centre of the yellow underparts. The great tit has a wide repertoire of distinctive calls, the best known being a metallic and bell-like "teechu-teechu-teechu", which is heard from January onwards. Common throughout Ireland, except in remote, treeless western areas and uplands, its preferred habitat is broad-leaved woodland, gardens and parks. There are about 420,000 pairs in the country. When they do not forage on the ground in search of food, they feed acrobatically in trees, hanging upside down to snatch insects from twigs or leaves. In winter and autumn, beech and other seeds are an important part of their diet. During this time, tits frequently band together in roaming flocks. Although they pioneered, along with blue tits (p.32), the opening of milk bottle tops to suck the cream, great tits also help gardeners by eating the caterpillars of the harmful winter moth. Irish great tits are generally sedentary, but will move some distance if there are local food shortages.

See 'Tits' p.30

Blue Tit

Parus caeruleus
Meantán gorm
VERY COMMON RESIDENT
11.5 CM

The blue tit is the only tit with bright blue in its plumage. The crown is cobalt-blue, surrounded by white, with a black eyestripe meeting behind the head. The cheeks are white and the underparts are sulphur-yellow. Young birds are a dull yellow-green, easily confused with warblers. Blue tits are common throughout Ireland, with about 1 million breeding pairs. They prefer broad-leaved woodland (especially oaks), hedgerows and gardens. Their commonest call note is "tsee-tsee-tsee-tsit", heard from early spring. Often very tame, they are regular visitors to bird tables. Sometimes they attack putty around windows and if they enter houses, they will often tear up strips of paper (even wallpaper) – a behaviour possibly related to pulling the bark off trees in search of insects. When nesting in woodlands, the breeding cycle is geared to coincide with the maximum abundance of caterpillars, which form their staple food. Blue tits breed less successfully in urban environments, a fact attributed to the poor nutritive value of bird-table food. Irish blue tits are sedentary, not moving very far from their natal areas. They will, however, join roaming flocks of tits in the autumn.

See 'Tits' p.30

ADULT

Coal Tit

Parus ater hibernicus

Meantán dubh

VERY COMMON RESIDENT

11.5 CM

ADULT

The coal tit is the smallest and the most brightly coloured of our four common tits. The large white patch on its black nape is a diagnostic feature. Irish coal tits belong to a special subspecies that differ from British and Continental coal tits by the yellowish tint of the white cheeks and the white nape patch. The Irish birds are also slightly smaller. However, there is much variation within the Irish population and the distinctions are not always that clear. Widespread across the country, with about 270,000 breeding pairs, the coal tit prefers woodland habitats, especially where there are conifers, but it is also found in gardens and parks – where it is normally encountered on the bird table. It is the shyest of tits to visit the bird table, where it is intimidated by larger birds. It has increased and extended its range in western areas due to afforestation programmes. Coal tits make a loud, pipping "seetoo-seetoo" call in spring to proclaim their presence. Its narrow bill is adapted to picking off insects between coniferous needles. The coal tit loses heat and energy quickly in winter and, consequently, needs to feed constantly during this period.

See 'Tits' p.30

Swallow

Hirundo rustica

Fáinleog

<small>COMMON SUMMER VISITOR, DECLINING</small>

<small>APRIL–OCTOBER</small>

17–19 CM

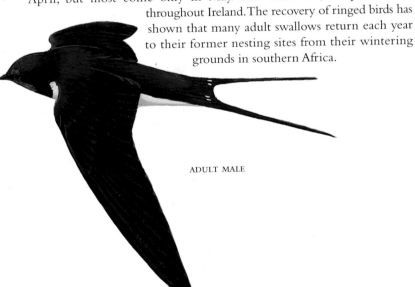

JUVENILE

The long tail streamers distinguish the swallow from the house (p.35) and sand martins (p.137) and the swift (p.36). Adult swallows have a chestnut-red throat and forehead, uniform dark blue upper parts, long wings and a forked tail. Their flight is buoyant, swift and swooping. They seldom alight on the ground except to pick up mud and grass nesting material. They sing a twittering song both on the wing and when perched on wires. They are held in special affection by man as harbingers of spring and also because of their close association with farm buildings for nest sites. The changes from traditional to modern farming may have been responsible for the recent declines in swallow numbers, as large flying insects such as hoverflies, bluebottles and horseflies are scarcer and buildings less accessible. Swallows start arriving in early April, but most come only in May. Less than 250,000 pairs breed throughout Ireland. The recovery of ringed birds has shown that many adult swallows return each year to their former nesting sites from their wintering grounds in southern Africa.

ADULT MALE

House Martin

Delichon urbica
Gabhlán binne
COMMON SUMMER VISITOR
APRIL–OCTOBER
12 CM

House martins have a distinctive white rump, contrasting with their blue-black backs and wings. Their tail is short, forked and without streamers. They are more sociable than swallows and their characteristic chirping call "prrt" heralds their presence. With about 70,000 breeding pairs, they are widespread. They occur more frequently than swallows in the urban areas, and stay away from the exposed areas of the counties - such as Donegal, Mayo and Galway - where winds, rain and low temperatures do not favour insect food, which is caught on the wing. Highest densities occur in eastern Ireland. Generally, house martins fly and feed in the zone below swifts (p.36), which take small insects, and that above swallows (opposite), which fly low and eat larger insects. House martins are rarely on the ground except to collect nesting material, to be fashioned into mud cups placed under eaves of buildings in small colonies. There are several cases of cliff-nesting in Ireland. The first birds arrive from their southern and tropical African wintering grounds in early April, but the bulk of birds do not appear until May. They are thought to be declining in numbers, though hard proof is difficult to obtain.

ADULT

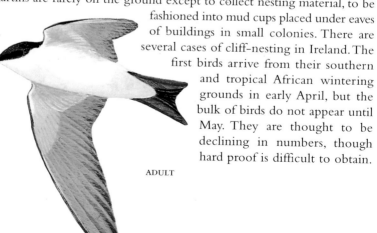

ADULT

Swift

Apus apus
Gabhlán gaoithe
COMMON SUMMER VISITOR
MAY–AUGUST
16–17 CM

No bird is more aerial in its lifestyle than the swift. Their long scythe-like wings, short forked tails, sooty-brown plumage and screaming, dashing flight distinguish swifts from swallows and martins. Sometimes they are called "Devil Birds" because of their black plumage. Their presence is emphasised by their low-flying, screaming displays around buildings, visible in May. They are totally dependent upon aerial insects and do not return from their African wintering grounds until early May, when there are sufficient small flies available. They are commonest in built-up areas, where they prefer tall buildings, such as Georgian houses, and nest in holes under the roofs. About 20,000 pairs breed in Ireland. They are scarce in exposed and windy western regions, where sufficient food cannot be guaranteed. Unique among Irish birds, they copulate on the wing (and again on the nest for good measure), with the non-incubating birds spending the night on the wing, sleeping in short snatches, and returning at dawn. The growth rate of the young in the nest is controlled, more than for any other bird, by weather conditions. Fledging takes 35 days in warm dry summers and up to 56 days in cold and windy conditions.

ADULT

Waxwing

Bombycilla garrulous
Síodeiteach

SCARCE LOCAL WINTER VISITOR (DECEMBER–MARCH). OCCASIONALLY IRRUPTIVE
18 CM

JUVENILE

The waxwing, about the size of a starling, has an unmistakable pinkish-chestnut crest on the head. Overall plumage colouration is a vinaceous-brown, and the birds are unique amongst western Palaearctic passerines in having both a head crest and bright-coloured "waxy" appendages on the secondary wing feathers. They have a black bib, grey rump and a rich brown vent. The black tail has a terminal yellow band. Their call, a sibilant trilling, is diagnostic. Waxwings breed in the sub-arctic and boreal regions of Fenno-Scandia, Estonia and Russia. Partial migrants, they are subject to massive population irruptions bringing thousands of birds into western Europe and some stragglers into Ireland. The irruptions are probably triggered by a successful breeding season, exacerbating food shortages and driving the birds into new areas in search of food. Some evidence also suggests 10-year population cycles. During an irruption, flocks of up to 50 birds appear in Dublin's urban areas, particularly parks and gardens, as well as in other east-coast conurbations. Some birds even make it to the west coast - for instance, in 1996 (a good "waxwing year") they visited Galway City; Kilkee and Ballyvaughn, Co. Clare; and Tralee and Listowel, Co. Kerry. During winter they feed mainly on berries, especially hawthorn, rowan and cotoneaster, generally swallowed whole. Waxwings sometimes eat 2-3 times their body weight on a daily basis.

ADULT

Farmland and Hedgerows

Extensive hedgerow landscape, Co. Wicklow. Much of Ireland's hedgerow landscape remains intact and provides valuable breeding habitat for yellowhammers, blackbirds, robins, dunnocks, and chaffinches. In winter the fruits and berries are important for visiting flocks of thrushes. (Photo: Redmond Cabot)

Until the 1970s, Ireland remained a sort of frozen agricultural landscape, with a long history of rural emigration. There were few signs of intensive farming outside certain areas in the east, south-east and south. As a consequence, hedgerows remained intact; rough land and small wetlands were left untouched; and scrubs and small woodlands survived. Ireland's entry into the European Union (EU) in 1973 brought about a change that produced both good and bad environmental consequences for bird life. On the one hand, the encouragement of overstocking of sheep spelt the demise of many fragile habitats such as upland moorlands and coastal machair grasslands, while some major wildfowl wetlands were finally destroyed through the completion of arterial drainage schemes. On the other hand, the EU agricultural support system lent a helping hand to farmers.

Drumlin landscape with a diversity of habitats – ponds and marshes in the hollows, hedgerows, open grassland and small plantations. Such habitats allow for balanced bird populations.

stay on the land so that the rich and varied rural fabric of small holdings, most of which are below 33 hectares in size, was maintained. Such a diverse structure of the landscape is beneficial to bird populations.

Another long-term change in the farming landscape has been the decline in the amount of land under cultivation for grain crops and tillage. In 1841, approximately 16 million hectares were under cultivation, including 8.7 million hectares under grain crops. By 1974, the amount of land under grain crops was only 2.18 million hectares. Today, Ireland's agricultural landscape is dominated by grassland supporting large numbers of cattle and sheep. The EU-supported Rural Environmental Protection Scheme (REPS), introduced during the mid-1990s, aims to encourage, through grants, more environmentally friendly farming. In the long run, REPS should benefit bird populations, but to what extent remains to be seen.

Changes in farming practices towards maximising this massive grass crop have meant that grass is cut earlier in the season to make silage. A variety of countryside birds have suffered from these changes, such as the corncrake, which nests in grass meadows and cannot breed securely anymore. The reduction of land under grain crops has also taken its toll on the partridge and the quail, which feed on grain and do not find enough to sustain their populations. The yellowhammer and the now extinct corn bunting are also victims of this declining availability of grain for food. Other birds, however, are thriving in this modern agricultural landscape. Grassland pasture provides rich food resources of beetle larvae, earthworms, wireworms and many other invertebrates quickly exploited by the rook (which occurs in higher densities here than in Britain), by the jackdaw and the starling. Birds feeding on carrion, such as the raven and the hooded crow, have also been prospering on sheep casualties, while magpies continue their dramatic expansion. These species are so frequently seen that visitors are surprised at the number of "black birds" which appear to be taking over the Irish countryside.

There has been little clearance of hedgerows, and this has benefited species such as the robin, blackbird, song thrush, chaffinch, long-tailed tit and yellowhammer, which use this habitat for nesting and shelter. During the winter months, the mosaic of hedgerow and extensive grass pastureland presents the ideal habitat for visiting fieldfares, redwings, blackbirds, chaffinches and the less frequent bramblings.

Highly mobile and single-minded in their pursuit of food, birds will seek out any new or alternative food source that presents itself in the evolving agricultural landscape. Waterfowl will partly forego their usual estuarine habitats with limited resources to graze some nearby improved grassland. The Wexford Slobs, Co. Wexford, are a classic example of this phenomenon, where new food opportunities arising in the aftermath of land reclamation attracted an increasingly larger population of wintering wildfowl from Greenland, Iceland and northern Europe. The Greenland white-fronted geese will take up the left-over and spilt grain in the autumn before switching to grass pastureland, but they will also exploit sugar beet if available. Brent geese, which are normally happy to feed on the eel grass while supplies last, and on sea lettuce in the adjacent harbour, will also come on to the Slob grasslands to graze, as will Bewick's swans, attracted to sugar beet and grass.

Abandoned farm, near Achill Island, Co. Mayo. Poorly drained and rush-ridden soil. Good for feeding curlew and snipe, especially in the drains, while hooded crows nest in isolated trees.

The development amongst farmers of a more benign attitude towards birds of prey, coupled with the prohibition of strychnine as a poison in 1992 and a significant reduction in the use of organochlorine pesticides, has taken some pressure off the kestrel, sparrowhawk and peregrine. They seem to be more frequent in the countryside, and birdwatchers are much more likely to encounter a peregrine than twenty years ago. Buzzards, as their increasing population shows, have also benefited greatly from the absence of strychnine.

Kestrel

Falco tinnunculus

Pocaire gaoithe

COMMON RESIDENT

32–35 CM

ADULT
FEMALE

Kestrels are distinguished from other Irish birds of prey by their habitual hovering behaviour. Their pointed wings separate them from the more rounded wings of the sparrowhawk (p.66). The male kestrel has a bluish-grey head, rump and tail which has a marked subterminal black band. The upper parts are black-spotted brown. The female is a uniform rufous brown, with dark brown bars which extend across the tail. When not hovering, they are often seen perched upright on posts or fences looking for prey. They execute a slanting descent from hovering to pounce on a field mouse or an insect, many of which are injurious to agriculture. Their call is a shrill "kee-kee-kee-kee". No nest is built, but a scrape is made on the ledge of a cliff. Sometimes, they settle in abandoned nests of crows or other large birds, where 4-6 eggs are laid. Incubation is mainly carried out by the female, who is fed by prey brought by the male. During winter, some birds from the upland areas may move to lowlands. Some Irish birds emigrate south, while others visit the country from Luxembourg, Belgium and Norway. There are about 10,000 breeding pairs in Ireland, widely distributed throughout the territory.

See 'Birds of Prey' p. 92

ADULT MALE

Pheasant

Phasianus colchicus
Piasún
VERY COMMON RESIDENT
53–89 CM

Male pheasants are copper-coloured, with a metallic dark green head and neck, red wattles surrounding the eye and a characteristically long tail. Females are much drabber and clad in warm brown. Pheasants are frequently seen crossing roads or on verges or feeding in fields. They are shy and wary. When disturbed, they prefer to run off but sometimes fly, taking off explosively in a whirring flight punctuated with short glides. The Caucasian pheasant was first introduced to Ireland in the late 16th century, followed by the Chinese pheasant – distinguished from its predecessor by a white neck ring – in the 18th century. The latter now dominate the wild breeding population. Males can have a harem of up to 20 females, but more ordinarily pair with only 2 or 3 which they protect. On average, 11 eggs are laid in a nest on the ground under vegetation and the chicks are led away on hatching. Hand-bred birds meet with poor breeding success, and when interbred with the wild population, productivity is even further reduced. Most hand-bred birds are shot within 400 m of the release point, with less than 1 per cent travelling more than 2 km. They are widely distributed throughout Ireland, with about 570,000 females and 530,000 males.

ADULT MALE

ADULT FEMALE

Stock Dove

Columba oenas

Colm gorm

FAIRLY COMMON RESIDENT

32—34 CM

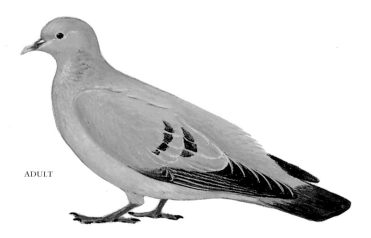

ADULT

The stock dove has a grey and black plumage and is distinguished from the rock dove (p.179) by the absence of a white rump. It also lacks the white neck patch and wing markings of the woodpigeon (opposite). It can be confused with feral pigeons, which often do not have a white rump. Up close, irridescent green patches can be seen on either side of the bird's neck. Its flight is quicker and more dashing than the woodpigeon's, and they are less gregarious. In winter, they generally occur in flocks, comprising less than 50 individuals. There are up to 30,000 breeding pairs in lowland, wooded agricultural areas, mostly concentrated in the grain-growing regions of the south and east, with the largest numbers in the counties of Meath, Louth, Kildare, Carlow and Kilkenny. Since colonising Ireland in the second half of the 19th century, they have gradually spread south of a line, stretching from Limerick to Dundalk in response to a higher proportion of arable farming there. They are often overlooked by ornithologists, but there is some evidence to suggest that their breeding range is now contracting. Irish birds are sedentary, with little evidence of immigration of British or Continental birds.

ADULT

Woodpigeon

Columba palumbus
Colm coille
VERY COMMON RESIDENT
40–42 CM

The woodpigeon is the largest of our pigeons and doves. Essentially blue-grey and plump-looking, they have a conspicuous white patch on the sides of the neck (lacking in young birds) and a white band across each wing. Theirs is a strong direct flight with a loud clapping of wings when leaving a tree and their song is an unmistakable "coo-cooo-coo-coo-coo". During display flight, the woodpigeons fly up steeply, clapping their wings noisily several times before descending again. They feed mostly on the ground and are serious agricultural pests, consuming large amounts of cereal crops, clover, brassicas and peas, among others. With 800,000–970,000 pairs, they are widespread throughout the country and have been increasing during the last 150 years. They have even become resident in some of the more remote western areas in the past 35 years. Despite various attempts and different methods, no satisfactory system has been developed to control numbers. Both adults feed the young on "pigeon milk" produced by special cells in the crop. Most Irish-bred birds are sedentary, but are joined by some winter immigrants from Britain and the Continent.

JUVENILE

ADULT

Barn Owl

Tyto alba
Scréachóg reilige
UNCOMMON RESIDENT, DECLINING
33–35 CM

ADULT

For an agricultural country not yet suffering such intensification as other neighbouring states, it is surprising how rare it is to see a barn owl. They are most likely observed at dusk as a ghostly white form, flitting low across the agricultural landscape or at night, illuminated in the headlights of a car. Mostly found in eastern Ireland, they are more likely to be encountered south of a line, stretching from Galway to Dundalk, where the majority of the estimated 150-200 pairs occur, most in lowlands below 100m. The greatest concentrations are in Cos. Kilkenny and Cork. The palest of the three owls are to be seen in Ireland, their upper parts are orange-buff, and their face and underparts are pure white. Their legs dangle behind them in a flight which is buoyant, wavering and totally silent. The barn owl locates its prey – field mice and brown rats – by acute directional hearing and its call is a long, drawn-out eerie shriek. It nests in hollow trees, old farm buildings, church towers and most recently, in boxes erected to encourage its expansion. A decline in numbers is almost certainly linked to the use of pesticides, which depress breeding success and survival. Most are sedentary, with dispersal of the young by the end of September.

ADULT

Rook

Corvus frugilegus
Rúcach
VERY COMMON RESIDENT
44–46 CM

Rooks are glossy black with a slender greyish bill, at the base of which is a bare whitish patch. They are an integral part of the Irish agricultural landscape, with about 520,000 breeding pairs scattered throughout the countryside and mostly occurring in rookeries of 50 pairs or fewer. Rooks are extremely sociable and highly gregarious. Their bulky twig nests are built in treetops (elms and Scots pines are favourites) and a rookery in early spring is alive with loud and raucous "cawing". Their social behaviour led some early naturalists to believe they held "rook parliaments" to adjudicate on twig-thieving behaviour. Although rooks will sometimes feed on cereals and potatoes, on balance they are beneficial to farming, eating many harmful insects such as wireworms and leatherjackets. In winter, they are likely to roost communally with jackdaws and travel to roost in the evening along fixed flight lines after a day spent eating out. Irish rooks are resident and rather sedentary, but there is probably some immigration of British rooks into Ireland in the autumn.

ADULT

ADULT

Hooded Crow

Corvus corone
Caróg liath
VERY COMMON RESIDENT
45–47 CM

ADULT

The hooded crow is easily distinguished from other crows by its grey back and underparts, contrasting with the rest of its all-black body. Frequent encounters with hooded crows are usually the first ornithological surprise for visitors to Ireland, as they are rare elsewhere in western Europe outside Denmark and Scotland. The hooded crow evolved as a colour variant of the black European crow, when the population was split and isolated during the last glaciation period. The crows then moved northwards, following the retreating ice, with the "black" or carrion crow occupying western Europe, and the newly evolved "grey" crow remaining in eastern and north-eastern Europe with a south-western "outpost" population extending down into Denmark, Scotland and Ireland. Widespread throughout Ireland with about 290,000 pairs, they are highly adaptable and successful. They feed on carrion, scavenge rubbish dumps, rob many bird eggs and snatch the young. On the coastline, the hooded crow breaks open shellfish by dropping them onto rocks. Family parties are quite commonly seen at the end of the summer. Some large winter roosts have been recorded totalling up to 167 individuals.

ADULT

Corncrake

Crex crex

Traonach

SCARCE LOCAL SUMMER VISITOR, DECLINING

APRIL–SEPTEMBER

27–30 CM

ADULT MALE

Seldom seen as it spends most of its time concealed in vegetation, the corncrake's presence is revealed by a loud rasping "crek-crek," persistently repeated day and night. Corncrakes are shy, but can be called out quite successfully by drawing a smooth bone across a notched one. A crepuscular bird, most active at dusk and night, the corncrake has a yellow-buff plumage, and conspicuous, rounded chestnut wings. Its flight is low and fluttering, with legs dangling behind. Its favourite habitat used to be hay fields, but it is now mainly found in damp pastureland areas, such as the River Shannon and the River Moy, Co. Mayo, catchments, a few isolated districts in west Mayo, north Donegal and on a few western islands. The corncrake population has been declining for years, and this bird is now in danger of extinction. In 1978, 1,500 males were recorded calling in the whole of Ireland; 903 in 1988 and only 132 in 2003. Corncrake management in Ireland, albeit in its early stages, has failed to evoke a population response so far, probably because mortality factors in its wintering grounds in south-east Africa and on the migration routes are working against the species.

AREA	1988	1993	1998	1999	2000	2001	2002	2003
North Donegal	310	46	63	74	76	80	99	82
West Connaught	256	30	17	16	14	20	20	27
Shannon Callows	125	88	69	65	58	54	20	22
Rest of Irish Republic ★	90	1	2	(1)	(4)	(4)	(3)	(6)
County Fermanagh	65	8	1	1	0	0	0	0
Rest of Northern Ireland	57	1	1	1	1	0	0	1
Total	903	174	153	157	149	154	139	132

NOTE: ★ *Only core areas are censused annually, so this figure is given for the national census years.*
The figures in brackets relate to reports of singing male corncrakes that were not confirmed but are considered to be reliable, although they are not included in the total for Ireland.
Source: Alex Copland, Birdwatch Ireland.

Golden Plover

Pluvialis apricaria

Feadóg bhuí

SCARCE LOCAL BREEDER, DECLINING. COMMON WINTER VISITOR (SEPTEMBER–APRIL)

26–29 CM

The golden plover is a medium-sized, brownish plover which sometimes seems to melt into the background when standing and sitting in winter flocks on rough ground. Its upper parts are dark brown, with a gold and black spangled pattern of markings; its underparts are buff-coloured. In summer plumage, the golden plover presents a black face and underparts boarded by a conspicuous white area, giving it a smart appearance. Solitary during the breeding season, they form large wheeling flocks in winter from September to April, to be seen in coastal areas and on open agricultural land. Their flight is swift with rapid wingbeats and flocks moving in unison. They exhibit typical plover feeding behaviour on the ground – short run, stop, pick up food, run, stop. Their typical call is a mournful "flui". Breeding numbers have decreased in recent years, probably as a result of afforestation and bog developments. An estimated 300–350 pairs breed (2002) in the lowland and upland bogs of Connemara, west Mayo and west Donegal (55 pairs were found during 2002, of which 21 were breeding on lowland blanket bog below 200 m – most unusual at such a low altitude). Up to 200,000 birds migrate from Iceland to Ireland in the winter.

See 'Waders' p.192

ADULT SUMMER

Lapwing
Vanellus vanellus
Pilibín

RESIDENT, DECLINING. COMMON WINTER VISITOR (OCTOBER–MARCH)
28–31 CM

ADULT

The lapwing is a very characteristic bird of the agricultural landscape during both the winter and the breeding seasons, when 2,000–5,000 pairs occur throughout Ireland. It is a greenish-black and white plover, with broad, rounded wings, a short tail and a slow, buoyant flight. Lapwings have a conspicuous crest and their gait is a short run, with frequent stops to pick up food by tilting their body forward without bending their legs. Their flight, especially during courtship, is wildly erratic with sudden dives, tumbles, swoops and twists. Their call is a loud "pee-wit". During winter, lapwings gather in large flocks, but by mid-March, they are back on their breeding grounds – rough pasture, grassland and sometimes arable fields – where the male makes several scrapes on the ground by sinking down on his breast, his feet scraping the soil. The female chooses one and completes it. The first eggs are laid in March, replacements in May and June. The lapwing mostly eats insects and will take a quota of wireworms and leatherjackets from the fields. Continental birds immigrate to Ireland, especially during harsh weather. Some Irish birds migrate south.
See 'Waders' p.192

ADULT MALE SUMMER

Curlew

Numenius arquata

Crotach

LOCAL RESIDENT, RECENT DECLINING
COMMON WINTER VISITOR (JULY–MARCH)
50–60 CM

ADULT

The curlew is the largest and most familiar of wading birds. Very much a bird characteristic of Ireland, it has a widespread and abundant distribution, stimulated by suitable lowland agricultural habitats. The curlew is easily identified by a streaky brown plumage, a long curved bill, long legs, and when in flight, a white rump. Named after its melancholy "coor-li" call, it also has a musical bubbling song on the breeding grounds. A shy and wary bird not allowing close approach, it has a swift and confident flight, often high before suddenly descending to the ground in a manner similar to the golden plover (p.50). It may be distinguished from the smaller whimbrel (p.205) by the latter's shorter bill, black-streaked crown and fairly different call. An estimated 1,000–3,000 pairs bred on moorland, lowland bog and lowland rough agricultural ground in 2002. After breeding, the birds gather in July-August along the coast, although many stay inland. When present along the coastline, they eat ragworm, crabs, sandhoppers, molluscs and shrimps, and in wet pastures, they turn to insects, larvae and earthworms. Large numbers from Scotland, northern England and Scandinavia winter in Ireland, with birds arriving as early as August.

See 'Waders' p.192

ADULT

Cuckoo

Cuculus canorus

Cuach

SUMMER VISITOR, PROBABLE DECREASE
(APRIL–AUGUST)

32–34 CM

JUVENILE

The cuckoo normally arrives during the second half of April, the earliest record being 2 April. Between 3,000 and 6,000 pairs visit Ireland each year. Akin to male sparrowhawks (p.66) in aspect, cuckoos have wings that are more pointed, a longer white-tipped tail and a low, dodging flight. Both sexes have similar blue–grey underparts and breast, while the whitish underparts are barred with darker markings. When perched, the cuckoo has a horizontal, rather than an erect, hawk-like profile, and only the male calls "coo-coo" when courting. Cuckoos are more frequent west of the River Shannon, numbers having decreased in the east, possibly due to a reduction in the numbers of their main host, the meadow pipit. After mating, the female cuckoo removes one egg from her victim's nest – the meadow pipit is the chief host species in Ireland – and lays a replacement within 10 seconds. This is repeated 10–20 times during the breeding season. Once hatched, the naked and blind baby cuckoo ejects all the other eggs and grabs the attention of its foster parents. Meanwhile, parent cuckoos have migrated south to Africa, leaving their young to follow in July and August, a behaviour demonstrating the remarkable quality of innate navigational instincts.

ADULT MALE

Skylark

Alauda arvensis

Fuiseog

VERY COMMON RESIDENT

COMMON WINTER VISITOR (SEPTEMBER–MARCH)

18–19 CM

ADULT

The skylark is a small streaky brown lark with buffish-white underparts, a boldly streaked breast and white outer tail feathers. It has a small head crest and walks in a crouched position. Skylarks have a characteristic soaring, musical outpouring sustained during ascent, hovering and descent. They are often seen taking dust baths. A widely distributed bird, with over half a million pairs breeding in Ireland, the skylark is found on farmland, rough grasslands, salt marshes, sand dunes and moorland. Outside the breeding season, it is gregarious and forms small flocks. As a breeding bird, it is most abundant west of the River Shannon, but during the winter, skylarks move to the richer agricultural lands in the east and south, creating a pronounced absence of birds from many western areas and several Midland regions. Large numbers of immigrants arrive in eastern Ireland from Europe in the autumn, but there is no evidence from recovery of ringed birds to show emigration of Irish-bred skylarks. Movements observed in the autumn along the south and eastern coasts may be Continental birds passing through.

ADULT

Meadow Pipit

Anthus pratensis

Riabhóg mhóna

VERY COMMON RESIDENT

WINTER VISITOR AND PASSAGE MIGRANT (SEPTEMBER–APRIL)

14.5CM

Superficially similar to the skylark (opposite) as well as occupying the same wide range of habitats, the meadow pipit is another small, streaky brown bird with white outer tail feathers. However, it is a smaller and leaner bird, definitely a pipit. Calling a distinctive thin "tseep", the meadow pipit also has a characteristic song delivered during ascent and then during a parachute descent with uplifted wings. With nearly a million breeding pairs in Ireland, the meadow pipit's adaptability allows it into all habitats, but it is a double victim of predation as the merlin's favourite food and the cuckoo's principal host. Recent afforestation has created abundant new habitat which, however, ceases to to be attractive when the plantation reaches six years of age. There is a large immigration of British, and possibly Continental, birds during September and October. Birds ringed on the south coast during this period have been recovered in Spain, France and Portugal. Whether these were Irish-bred or of Continental origin is not known.

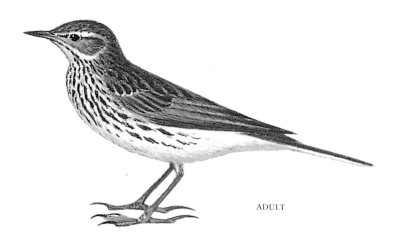

ADULT

THRUSHES

Blackbird (p.19), song thrush (p.20), fieldfare (p.57), redwing (p.58), mistle thrush (p.59) and ring ouzel (p.101)
• are roughly blackbird size
• feed on the ground, on worms and insects, and on berry-bearing trees and shrubs
• are mainly residents or winter visitors (ring ouzel is a summer visitor)
• most are gregarious outside the breeding season
• sexes are alike or nearly so
• habitat, season, behaviour, general colouration and the presence of distinctive coloured areas are all helpful in identification

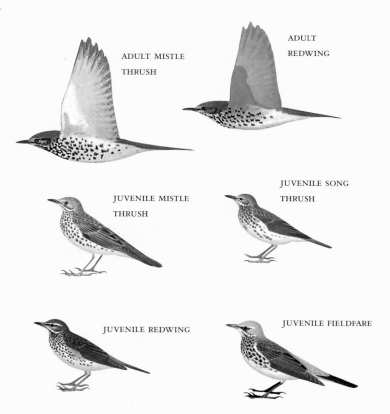

ADULT MISTLE THRUSH

ADULT REDWING

JUVENILE MISTLE THRUSH

JUVENILE SONG THRUSH

JUVENILE REDWING

JUVENILE FIELDFARE

Fieldfare

Turdus pilaris

Sacán

COMMON WINTER VISITOR

OCTOBER–APRIL

25.5 CM

The arrival of the fieldfare as a winter visitor from Scandinavia is determined by the exhaustion of the rowanberry crop in Norway and Sweden. Once the rowan crop is exhausted, fieldfares move south-west to Britain and Ireland, arriving from early October onwards with large immigrations in November. Loose flocks of 100 or more birds flying leisurely to the accompaniment of their loud "chacking" calls is a common November sight, especially east of the River Shannon. Further west and noticeably in west Donegal, Mayo and Galway, the birds are much less common. The fieldfare is larger than the other Scandinavian winter visitor the redwing (p.58) and has a slate-grey nape and rump. The back is chestnut and the tail is black. The grey rump and white "flashing" underwings are good field characteristics in flight. Their noisy "tchak-tchak-tchak" call is also unmistakable. They are birds of open country, preferring rough pasture, where they occur in small straggly flocks, often very noisy and with an upright stance. They feed on insects. Fruit and berries are also taken. The fieldfare is very nomadic and subject to hard weather movements.

See 'Thrushes' p.56

ADULT

ADULT WINTER

Redwing

Turdus iliacus
Deargán sneachta
COMMON WINTER VISITOR
OCTOBER–APRIL
21 CM

The redwing is the smallest of our thrushes and our commonest winter visitor from northern Europe and Iceland. It is distinguished from the similar song thrush (p.20) by a creamy eye stripe and chestnut-red flanks and underwing. In flight, the red underwing is distinctive. Redwings have a high-pitched and plaintive "seeip" call, often heard at night as birds fly overhead on migration from Scandinavia. They are gregarious, feeding in loose flocks, often mixed with fieldfares (p.57), roaming the countryside in search of food. Open agricultural landscape with hedgerows and small woodlands is their favoured habitat. They feed on berries of hawthorn, rowan, holly and yew, but also on worms, snails and many different insects. Redwings are more widely distributed throughout Ireland than fieldfares. They occur less frequently in west Donegal, west Mayo, west Galway and in west Kerry and upland areas. They will often visit gardens where contoneaster berries are on offer. The bulk of wintering redwings comes from Scandinavia, with some Icelandic visitors in their wake. Breeding was attempted in Kerry (1951).

See 'Thrushes' p.56

ADULT

ADULT WINTER

Mistle Thrush

Turdus viscivorus

Liatráise

COMMON RESIDENT

27 CM

ADULT

The mistle thrush is distinguished from the song thrush (p.20) by its greyish-brown upper parts and its bolder markings consisting of bigger and broader spots on the underparts. They have a strong, direct flight, usually higher than the blackbird and song thrush, with a pronounced closure of their wings. They spend much of their time on grassy fields, standing upright, bold and alert while looking for food. Mistle thrushes are resident and widespread across the country, particularly in open areas featuring tall trees, and have a breeding population of some 90,000 pairs. Solitary nesters, they occur in widely spaced pairs, sometimes taking up residence in larger gardens or parks. Their nest is bulky and usually placed high in the bare fork of a tree. Parent birds are quite defensive of their territory and do not let themselves be intimidated by magpies or crows. Their song is loud, with repeated phrases similar to the blackbird, but lacking mellowness. The normal call is a rasping "tuc–tuc–tuc". Astonishingly, the mistle thrush was not found in Ireland before 1800, when the first one was shot in County Antrim. Colonisation was rapid, and by 1850, it was recorded in all counties. Birds bred in Scotland and northern England winter in Ireland.

See 'Thrushes' p.56

ADULT

Goldfinch

Carduelis carduelis
Lasair choille
COMMON RESIDENT
12 CM

ADULT

The goldfinch is a striking, jaunty finch with black and
yellow wings and a red and white pattern on its head.
The young are streaky brown with yellow–white wing
patches. Their canary-like song is a liquid twittering and
they have a flitting, dancing flight. With about 55,000 breeding pairs across
Ireland, they are fairly widespread in the open agricultural landscape and
gardens, especially where there are some trees and patches of weeds.
Neglected farmland is particularly favoured. Their long, thin bill allows
access into thistle heads, knapweed and teasels to extract seeds, which are
an important part of their diet. There was a serious decline of goldfinches
during the 19th century, when many were caught for the birdcage trade.
Numbers increased again after bird protection laws were passed in the
1930s, but there is some evidence that the population has decreased since
1968. However, the goldfinch still breeds in every county. Outside the
breeding season, it is very sociable, joining small roaming groups of up to
100 birds. There is some immigration of British-bred goldfinches in the
autumn, but it is not clear whether any Irish-bred birds migrate to the
Continent. Comparisons between known breeding and wintering
distributions in Ireland would suggest some emigration.

See 'Finches' p.21

ADULT

Yellowhammer

Emberiza citrinella
Buíóg
LOCALLY COMMON RESIDENT, DECLINING
16–16.5 CM

The male yellowhammer has a bright yellow head and underparts, a chestnut rump and white outer tail feathers. The female and juveniles are less yellow and duller. The yellowhammer's high-pitched song, translating as "a little bit of bread and no cheese" can be heard from a telegraph wire or a high perch in a hedge or tree. Formerly more widespread in agricultural landscapes featuring hedges, small bushes, trees and some open ground, its distribution has dramatically contracted since 1970, as many areas, which once had a good population, were deserted. Their decline is thought to be correlated with a decrease in the amount of land under tillage. Outside south-east Ireland and East County Donegal, there are only a few pockets where it is common. An estimated 10,000–40,000 pairs still breed in Ireland, and they are now of conservation concern. Their winter diet is mainly composed of cereal grains and large grass seeds. Birds tend to flock together in winter and there is no evidence from ringing recoveries of emigration. Large numbers of yellowhammers sometimes appear in the autumn in coastal areas, and are probably immigrants from northern Europe.

See 'Sparrows & Buntings' p.21

ADULT FEMALE
SUMMER

ADULT MALE
SUMMER

Woodland and Scrubland

Young plantation of sitka spruce and lodgepole pine. Ideal habitat for the expanding population of siskins, crossbills, goldcrests and long eared owls.

At the end of the 16th century, Ireland was densely stocked with woodlands, with nearly 13 per cent of forested country. The woodlands were broadleaved and dominated by oak. By 1800, these woodlands had been decimated by commercial exploitation, creating a naked landscape where only two per cent of the land surface was clothed by forest. Today, Ireland has only about nine per cent of land surface covered with trees, and is one of the least-wooded countries of Europe. Most of the woodland cover is in state ownership and is made up of two alien species, sitka spruce and lodgepole pine, both from North America. National afforestation programmes, which have lately gathered momentum – with 10,000 to 20,000 hectares of new coniferous forest planted every year, are generating the greatest ecological change to have occurred in Ireland in the last 50 years. While there are commercial reasons for coniferous plantations, many people regret the absence of extensive broad-leaved woodlands, which are more attractive to a diverse bird population.

Today, only about two per cent of the country is covered by deciduous woodland, much of it oak. Two detailed surveys of oakwoods in counties Kerry and Wicklow revealed that the most abundant species of birds (comprising up to 85 per cent of the breeding bird community) during the breeding season were chaffinches, robins, goldcrests, blue and coal tits and wrens. It often comes as a surprise to overseas visitors that many common woodland birds of our nearest neighbour, Britain, are absent from Ireland, arousing much speculation as to the ecological reasons why this should be so. The three woodpeckers, nuthatch, willow and marsh tits, tawny owl, nightingale and tree pipit are absent, while the redstart, pied flycatcher and wood warbler are extremely rare or scarce breeders. Visitors to Ireland also lament the scarceness of the blackcap, garden and willow warblers from apparently similar woodland habitat encountered in Britain. While Ireland is well within the geographical breeding range of the species listed above, many of which are summer migrants, a variety of ecological factors, including a lack of extensive broad-leaved woodlands are at work to deprive Ireland of a richer woodland bird life.

Well established broadleaved woodland near Lough Erne, Co. Fermanagh. Good for a diversity of warblers and some woodcock.

Classic oak woodland with understory of holly and rich growth of mosses, ferns and lichens, Co. Kerry. Favoured habitat of chaffinch, robin, blue and coal tits, goldcrest and wren.

In the meantime, however, while being unpopular for aesthetic and ecological reasons, the afforestation programme has opened up major new breeding habitats for many birds. These can be divided into two groups. A first group, including the hen harrier, sedge and grasshopper warblers, woodcock, whinchat and whitethroat, enjoys the nesting cover provided by the young growing trees. After six or seven years, however, the closing tree canopy changes the attractiveness of the shrub layer as a nesting and feeding habitat. The displaced birds then move on and colonise newly-planted sites, while a second group, including the crossbill, siskin, long-eared owl, goldcrest, coal tit and jay, moves into the maturing plantations to exploit the habitat offered by the tall trees.

Upland scrub oak-birch woodland with moorlands and gorse. Typical stonechat country in foreground with curlew, skylarks and meadow pipits on open moorland. Chaffinches and other usual woodland birds.

Sparrowhawk

Accipiter nisus

Spióróg

FAIRLY COMMON RESIDENT

28–38 CM

The sparrowhawk is distinguished from all other birds of prey by short, broad, rounded wings, a long tail, barred underparts and its method of hunting. The male has dark grey upper parts and rufous, barred underparts. The female is larger, with dark brown upper parts and brown barred whitish underparts. Both have long yellow legs. When hunting, the sparrowhawk has a dashing, low, almost jinking flight along hedges or through woodland. It will fly fast along a hedge, whip across to the other

ADULT FEMALE

side, either through a gap or straight over, and surprise a bird which it then grabs by its talons. If missed, the sparrowhawk rarely pursues its prey, moving on to another target. Although the commonest bird of prey, with an estimated 11,000 pairs breeding throughout Ireland in preferred wooded agricultural landscape, it is secretive, somewhat shy, and therefore less frequently seen than the kestrel (p.42). In high-quality habitats, densities are sometimes high, as evidenced by the seven pairs found in Phoenix Park, Dublin, an area of about 700 hectares. Sparrowhawks are sedentary, few birds travelling more than 30km from their natal areas.

See 'Birds of Prey' p.92

ADULT MALE

Buzzard

Buteo buteo

Clamhán

SCARCE LOCAL RESIDENT, RECENT INCREASE

51–57 CM

The buzzard has a characteristic soaring flight in wide circles, which will last for up to several hours as the bird quarters the landscape in search of prey ranging from rabbits and field mice to small birds and beetles. In silhouette, it has broad, rounded wings, with primary feather tips separating to give a finger-like appearance. The buzzard's neck is short, its tail is rounded and it utters a long "pee-oo" mew in flight or when perched. Its plumage is variable, but it generally has dark brown upper parts, mottled white underparts and the legs are bright yellow. Buzzards formerly bred in counties Antrim, Down, Donegal and Derry, on cliffs and in woods, but by the end of the 19th century, they had been persecuted to extinction. A small revival commenced in 1933 in Co. Antrim, but petered out. Breeding was re-established in 1966 and numbers have been generally increasing to reach about 200 pairs in Northern Ireland and about 150 pairs in the Republic, most of which are in Cos. Donegal, Louth, Monaghan and Wicklow. The Irish population may be supplemented by immigrants from Scotland, as indicated by three recoveries of young birds in Northern Ireland. Wandering birds are increasingly seen outside breeding areas.

See 'Birds of Prey' p.92

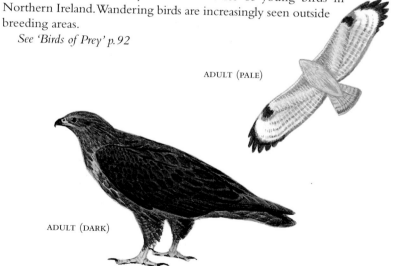

ADULT (PALE)

ADULT (DARK)

Woodcock

Scolopax rusticola
Creabhar
LOCAL RESIDENT. COMMON WINTER
VISITOR (OCTOBER–MARCH)
33–35 CM

ADULT

The woodcock is a solitary woodland species which, unless disturbed, is seldom seen. Similar to a large snipe (p.132) but plumper and with a thicker bill, it has more rounded wings and traverse black bars on the back of its head and neck. Taking off suddenly when startled, woodcock will drop into the undergrowth after a short dodging flight. Their well setback eyes and their cryptic plumage allow for all-round vision and concealment. From mid-February to July, woodcock enter an extraordinary territorial display flight or "roding" at dusk, when the male flies a regular circuit above the trees or the open ground, uttering two calls, a thin "tsiwick" and a low frog-like croak. Favouring damp, broad-leaved woods, they are also found in coniferous plantations and emerge at dusk to feed in nearby fields. Somewhere between 1,750–4,500 breeding pairs occur in suitable habitat throughout the country. Most Irish-bred woodcock are sedentary, although there have been recoveries of Irish young birds from Sweden, Scotland, England, France, Spain and Portugal. There is massive winter immigration in November from England and a wide area of Europe to the east of the Urals. Further influxes occur during severe weather.

See 'Waders' p.192

ADULT

Long-eared Owl

Asio otus

Ceann cait

LOCAL RESIDENT

WINTER VISITOR (SEPT–MAY)

33–35 CM

ADULT

These owls are seldom seen, as they spend the day roosting close to the trunk of a tree, cryptically concealed, only emerging at night to feed on their favourite prey, wood mice and brown rats. Their longer wings distinguish them from their close relative, the short-eared owl, which is a winter visitor from the Continent (October to April), regularly occurring in the open countryside, coastal areas and sand dunes during the day. Long-eared owls, however, reveal their presence from early January to early April by their long drawn-out "oo-oo-oo" call. Young birds in the nest and recently fledged birds make a loud and squeaky call reminiscent of a creaky gate. If seen, they have long ear tufts and buff plumage, with pale mottling and dark streaks. They are more frequent in the east than west, with 1,100–3,600 pairs, mostly in coniferous woodland. Most Irish birds are sedentary, the adults returning to the same breeding area, while the young move further away. Birds breeding in northern Europe migrate south and many come to Ireland.

ADULT

Hoopoe

Upupa epops

Húpú

<small>Rare passage migrant (mainly March–May).</small>

26–28 cm

The hoopoe is unmistakable – a veritable "jail" bird sporting boldly barred black and white wings and tail, set against a pinkish brown body plumage. The relatively large crest is erectable, its feathers tipped black. The bill is long (5–6cm), yellow and down turned, adapted for stabbing the ground, probing and grubbing up insect larvae. In flight, it is about the size of a jay, with the same kind of way of opening and closing of the wings, butterfly style. It is a ground feeder and can sometimes appear relatively tame. Hoopoes that turn up in Ireland are "overshoot" migrants, especially during anti-cyclonic weather conditions, from some 100,000 breeding pairs in France. Numbers recorded in Ireland each year are highly variable, with upwards of about 20 birds on average, except for three lean years during 1998–2000, when only a handful were observed. They mostly arrive in Cos. Cork, Wexford, Kerry, Waterford, and Wicklow. There have been 30 cases of breeding in Britain over the past 140 years, and it has been postulated that it will not be long before they attempt to nest in Ireland.

ADULT

ADULT

WARBLERS

Warblers
- are roughly tit-sized but with proportionately longer tails
- are very active insect eaters, with slender bills
- are all migratory, arriving April/May and mostly gone by September
- voice and habitat preference are important in identification

Usually in trees: chiffchaff (p.76) and willow warbler (p.77); the 'leaf warblers'
- greenish with eyestripe, sexes alike
- song is the most reliable means of identification
- can sometimes be confused with goldcrest (p.78)

Usually in scrub/thickets: whitethroat (p.73) and blackcap (p.75), garden (p.74) and wood warbler (p.74)
- sexes alike in garden warbler, nearly so in whitethroat, quite distinct in blackcap
- whitethroat colouring and song distinctive; blackcap and garden warbler songs alike but colours very different

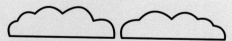

Usually in or near marshy ground: grasshopper warbler (p.72) and sedge warbler (p.140)
- streaky brown backs, sexes alike
- song is the most reliable means of identification

Grasshopper Warbler

Locustella naevia

Ceolaire casarnaí

FAIRLY COMMON SUMMER VISITOR, DECLINING

APRIL–OCTOBER

12.5 CM

This is a small, skulking and secretive warbler with a song similar to the sound of an angler's reel being wound in. This very distinctive song is often heard at night. The grasshopper warbler has olive-brown upper parts, with dark streaking, lightly streaked pale underparts and a well-rounded, slightly barred tail. It is somewhat similar to the sedge warbler (p.140), but distinguished by a different song and behaviour. Grasshopper warblers occupy a wide range of habitats, their favourite ones being overgrown and scrubby wasteland and young coniferous plantations. With about 5,500 breeding pairs, their main concentration occurs west of the River Shannon, while their numbers and breeding range in eastern Ireland seem to be contracting. Spring migrants generally arrive at the end of April and depart in early October to reach their winter quarters in tropical West Africa. The recent decline in numbers may be linked to ongoing desertification in the Sahel region.

See 'Warblers' p. 71

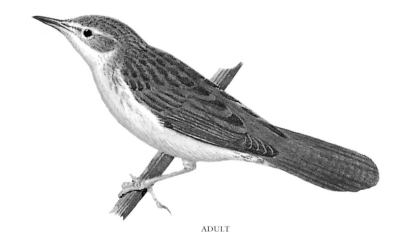

ADULT

Whitethroat

Sylvia communis

Gilphib

COMMON SUMMER VISITOR, DECLINING

APRIL–OCTOBER

14 CM

The whitethroat is another small, brownish warbler immediately distinguished by its rusty wings, long tail and white outer tail feathers. Male birds have a pale grey cap descending below the eye and a bright white throat. Females are brown-capped. The whitethroat's song is a brief and lively warble sung by the male, which is often perched high in a bush or in an exposed position. Frequently used contact notes include a harsh "tacc-tacc" and "charr". Nesting in a broad range of habitats, they are found in scrubland, bracken thickets, overgrown wasteland and young forestry plantations. Widespread throughout the country with 120,000 nesting pairs, whitethroats occur in greater numbers in the Midlands and also in the Burren, Co. Clare. A population crash occurred in 1969 due to the impact of desertification in the Sahel region, which lead to increased mortality of the wintering birds. Large areas in the south-west, such as Cos. Kerry, Cork and Limerick, as well as the north-eastern parts of Ireland, seem to have lost many breeding birds.

See 'Warblers' p. 71

ADULT MALE
SUMMER

Garden Warbler

Sylvia borin

Ceolaire garraí

SCARCE LOCAL SUMMER VISITOR. (MAY–OCTOBER) UNCOMMON PASSAGE MIGRANT IN SPRING AND AUTUMN

14 CM

ADULT

Medium-sized to large, plump warbler. Dull brown above and pale buff below, characteristic rounded head and stubby bill. Not easy to identify. Its song is a characteristic sustained, rich contralto warbling, reminiscent of a whitethroat, and a scolding "tchack". Migrants first arrive late April through May – regularly recorded at Great Saltee, Co. Wexford, Copeland Bird Observatory, Co. Down, and less frequently at Cape Clear Island, Co. Cork. The small breeding population, estimated at 330–400 pairs in 1991, is focussed in deciduous woodlands and scrub of the river Shannon lakes (principally Lough Ree), lower Lough Erne, Co. Fermanagh and Cavan lakes. Recorded nesting at many other locations from Cos. Cork to Donegal and Kerry to Wexford, as well as at Lough Neagh, where nesting ceased mid-1970s. Three sites in Co. Wicklow held up to seven singing males in 1998. Despite much available nesting habitat, the breeding population remains small.

Wood Warbler

Phylloscopus sibilatrix

Ceolaire coille

RARE LOCAL SUMMER VISITOR (APRIL–AUGUST) RARE PASSAGE MIGRANT (MAINLY APRIL–MAY) AND (AUGUST–SEPTEMBER)

12 CM

ADULT SPRING

A rare summer visitor and breeder, the wood warbler is an increasing, passage migrant. It is a small warbler with brightly contrasting, yellowish green upper-parts, yellow throat and breast and white belly. Again, it is best recognised by its song – a sad "piu" repeated about 20–30 times and a grasshopper-like song, a thinner and weaker version of the chaffinch's song. An estimated 2–20 pairs breed, many of which are in Co. Wicklow. Nesting also recorded in Cos. Mayo, Donegal, Antrim and Kerry, during 2000. Their preferred habitat is oak woodland.

Blackcap

Sylvia atricapilla

Caipín dubh

LOCAL SUMMER VISITOR (MAY–OCTOBER) PASSAGE MIGRANT AND UNCOMMON
WINTER VISITOR

13 CM

The glossy, black cap of the male and the red-brown cap of the female make blackcaps the easiest of the warblers to identify. Their scolding notes resemble those of the whitethroat (p.73), but a much more attractive song has earned them the appellation of "northern nightingales". Breeding in open, broad-leaved woodland with good ground cover, such as brambles and briar thickets, they were recorded in twenty-four counties at the end of the last century. This figure had contracted to six by the early 1960s (Cos. Wicklow, Cavan, Down, Antrim, Wexford and Limerick). Since then, the breeding range has extended again westwards and northwards, with some contraction east of the River Shannon. About 40,000 pairs breed in the country today. Increasing numbers of blackcaps, shown to be migrants from northern and eastern Europe, are wintering in suburban gardens in counties Antrim, Down, Dublin, Wicklow, Wexford and Cork, while the Irish blackcaps spend the cold season away in Africa.

See 'Warblers' p. 71

ADULT FEMALE
SUMMER

ADULT MALE
SUMMER

Chiffchaff

Phylloscopus collybita

Tiuf-teaf

WIDESPREAD SUMMER VISITOR

MARCH–OCTOBER

10–11 CM

The chiffchaff is a small, slim, graceful warbler, best identified by a distinctive song made up of two notes "chiff" and "chaff", repeated in various combinations. Similar to the willow warbler (opposite), it is slightly browner above and buffer below, and has a drabber appearance. Also, its legs are nearly always black, while the willow warbler's are pale. Chiffchaffs have a soft "hooeet" contact call while moving about in dense vegetation. They prefer broad-leaved woodlands lined with rich undergrowth, and establish song posts in tall trees. Widespread throughout Ireland, they are absent from a few treeless and sparse western areas. About 290,000 pairs of chiffchaffs breed in Ireland. The first spring migrants arrive from early March onwards, with birds departing at the end of August through September, to the end of October and a few stragglers leaving in November. Increasing numbers are wintering in Ireland, particularly along the south coast, but it is not known whether they are from the Continent or are Irish-bred birds.

See 'Warblers' p. 71

ADULT

Willow Warbler

Phylloscopus trochilus
Ceolaire sailí
WIDESPREAD SUMMER VISITOR
APRIL–OCTOBER
9–10 CM

The willow warbler is best identified by its characteristic song, which is fluent and wistful. It is a musical cadence starting off quietly and becoming firmer while descending to a final "sooeet-sooeeto" flourish. Sharing the same contact note as the chiffchaff (opposite), it is slightly more yellow-green in plumage and its legs are pale, not black. However, care should be taken, as the legs of some individuals can sometimes be black. Less dependent upon woodland than the chiffchaff, willow warblers are found in a wider range of habitats and are more broadly distributed and more numerous than the latter. There are approximately 830,000 pairs in Ireland, actively benefiting from the development of coniferous plantations. Densities of willow warblers are low in Irish oakwoods due to successful competition from goldcrests (p.78), as well as the lack of suitable undergrowth such as birch, which has been replaced in many instances by rhododendron. The first migrants arrive at the end of March and early April and depart in August/September, with a few stragglers in November. Unlike the chiffchaff, the willow warbler is not often recorded as overwintering.

See 'Warblers' p.71

ADULT SPRING

Goldcrest

Regulus regulus
Cíorbhuí
VERY COMMON RESIDENT. COMMON WINTER VISITOR (SEPTEMBER–MAY)
ALL YEAR
9 CM

Weighing only five grams, this is the smallest Irish bird. Diminutive in size, it has a plump form and a bright yellow crown with a black border. Its upper parts are olive-green and its underparts are buffish. Two white wing bars are noticeable in flight. A distinctive, high-pitched "zee-zee-zee" contact call – more than often issued from a coniferous tree – announces the goldcrest's presence, while its shrill song running "cedar-cedar-cedar-cedar-sissa-pee" can be heard from a great distance. Goldcrests are widespread and abundant birds in Ireland, with about 300,000 breeding pairs. Highest densities are found in broad-leaved and coniferous woods in the south, the Midlands, parts of the west and eastern Ireland. Only in the western fringes, which lack tree cover, are goldcrests not found. As with a number of Irish birds, afforestation programmes have opened up new habitats and allowed for a wider distribution. During October, there is a marked movement of birds in coastal areas, as some Continental goldcrests migrate to Ireland for the winter.

See 'Warblers' p. 71

JUVENILE

ADULT MALE

Spotted Flycatcher

Muscicapa striata

Cuilire liath

COMMON SUMMER VISITOR, RECENT DECLINE
(MAY–SEPTEMBER)

14.5 CM

JUVENILE

One of the most unobtrusive and nondescript Irish birds, the spotted flycatcher is also one of the latest comers of the spring migrants, which ensures it a good supply of insect food. It is probably best identified by its upright stance on a regular perch, with frequent sorties after flying insects – often caught with an audible snap – followed by the bird's return to the perch, a behaviour reminiscent of a chameleon in pursuit of flies. The spotted flycatcher's favoured habitats are edges of woods, farmyards, suburban gardens and parks. Both sexes have ashy-brown upper parts and lightly streaked, whitish breasts. They have an agile, almost ballet-like acrobatic flight, with wing and tail flicking when on their perch. Their call is a rasping "tzee", followed by a quick "tzee-tuc-tuc". The spotted flycatcher occurs throughout Ireland, with less than 35,000 breeding pairs and is most abundant in the Midlands and eastern areas. There has been a recent decline in numbers, especially in western and south-western regions. Birds depart Ireland in August and September for South Africa.

ADULT

Pied Flycatcher

Ficedula hypoleuca

Cuilire alabhreac

VERY RARE AND SPORADIC BREEDER (UP TO 5 PRS). (APRIL–SEPTEMBER) SCARCE
PASSAGE MIGRANT (APRIL–JUNE; SEPTEMBER–OCTOBER).

13 CM

The male is a striking black and white bird, the female olive-brown above
and buffish-white below. Both have a large white wing patch. Formerly
known as an autumn migrant, with a few appearing on spring passage
(Cape Clear, Co. Cork; Great Saltee, Co. Wexford and Tory Island, Co.
Donegal, are the best locations), they are a recently established breeding
species. One pair nested successfully in Breen Forest, Co. Antrim,
1985–1988, while two pairs bred unsuccessfully in Co. Wicklow, 1985.
Since then, odd pairs have bred spasmodically in the oak woods of Co.
Wicklow.

JUVENILE

ADULT MALE

Redstart

Phoenicurus phonenicurus

Earrdheargán

VERY RARE SUMMER VISITOR (APRIL–OCTOBER) SCARE PASSAGE MIGRANT
(APRIL–MAY AND AUGUST–OCTOBER)

14 CM

The redstart is also a very rare summer visitor and scarce breeder (5–20 pairs per year) in oak woods in Co. Wicklow and elsewhere. The male has an unusual plumage – a rusty orange tail, orange underparts, a black bib and grey head and back. The female is brown, with a rusty red tail. They have bred spasmodically in Co. Wicklow since 1885. From 1966 onwards, breeding numbers surged with regular nesting in the oak woods of Co. Wicklow and a scattering of records from Cos. Donegal, Antrim, Derry, Tyrone, Mayo and Kerry. They are also regular spring and autumn migrants on Great Saltee, Co. Wexford; Cape Clear Island, Co. Cork and the Copeland Islands, Co. Down.

ADULT
FEMALE

ADULT MALE

Long-tailed Tit

Aegithalos caudatus

Meantánerrfhada

COMMON RESIDENT

14 CM

These tits are easily identifiable by their small ball-like body of black, white and pinkish plumage and very long, narrow tail. Their call is of two kinds, an abrupt low "tupp" and a more tit-like "zee-zee-zee". Long-tailed tits are active birds, always seeming to be on the move, and very sociable ones. An estimated 40,000 pairs breed in woodland thickets, hedgerows and bushy areas on woodland edges throughout Ireland. They are inevitably absent from the treeless and windswept western parts of the country. Their nest is a domed construction, built by both sexes working from inside outwards. Mosses are elaborately woven together with cobwebs and some hair, while concealing lichens patch the outside, and over 2,000 feathers of many different kinds act as lining. If the nest is lost by predation, the male bird may "assist" another nest belonging to his brother or very close relative. In the autumn, family parties come together to form roaming bands of up to 50 birds, which work the woods and hedgerows for insect food. They are absent from many western areas during the winter, having moved to richer food habitats in the east and south.

See 'Tits' p.30

JUVENILE

ADULT

Treecreeper

Certhia familiaris
Snag
COMMON RESIDENT
12.5 CM

A small, inconspicuous, tree-climbing bird with a relatively long, curved bill, the treecreeper is the only Irish bird of its kind and the closest thing to an Irish woodpecker. The treecreeper's upper parts are brown, streaked with buff and its underparts are silvery-white but seldom seen, as the bird spends most of its time clinging to tree bark or branches in search of insects. Its contact call is a prolonged "tsee", while the song starts slowly and accelerates towards the end "tsee-tsee-tsee-wizzizu-ee". Broad-leaved or mixed woodlands are the treecreeper's favoured habitats. They nest in cracks behind the bark and prove very difficult to entice into a nest box. Widely scattered across Ireland with 45,000 pairs, their distribution remains patchy with a noticeable reduction over the past thirty years in Co. Wexford, north Cork and in the Midlands. The reasons for this are obscure. Treecreepers are amongst the most sedentary of Irish birds, and there is no evidence to suggest winter immigration from Britain or the Continent.

ADULT

JUVENILE

Jay
Garrulus glandarius hibernicus
Scréachóg
RESIDENT
34–35 CM

ADULT

The jay is an exotic-looking crow with a pinkish-brown body, blue and black barred wing coverts, a white rump and a white patch on the wing. Announcing its presence by a harsh loud "shraah-shraah", the jay is seldom seen outside broad-leaved or coniferous woodlands and is difficult to approach. When seen, it is usually flying away, revealing its pure white rump. Irish jays belong to a special subspecies, which has darker and more rufous sides to the head, ear coverts, breast and flanks. Their forehead and crown are usually darker, with broader, black streaks. However, some experts consider the Irish jay indistinguishable from the British form. A local breeder with an estimated 10,000 pairs in Ireland, the jay has apparently been extending its range northwards and westwards since the beginning of the century, while becoming scarcer in the south-east, where its absence from suitable breeding habitats is difficult to explain. During the winter, jays are usually sedentary and feed on acorns.

ADULT

Siskin

Carduelis spinus

Siscin

COMMON RESIDENT INCREASING WINTER VISITOR
(SEPTEMBER–MAY)

12 CM

ADULT
FEMALE

The male siskin is clad in striking yellow-green, with
a black crown and chin and a yellow rump. The wings
have yellow bars, as do the sides of the tail. The female
is duller, with less yellow and no black on the head.
Because of their general behaviour and explosive calls,
siskins can evoke restless and noisy cagebirds to the observer. Their
characteristic flight note is a shrill "tsy-zi", which will announce a bird in
flight or perched in coniferous trees. A former winter visitor, the siskin
started to breed in Ireland at the end of last century, and its recent rapid
expansion is a consequence of afforestation opening up vast breeding and
feeding grounds. They are particularly abundant in Cos. Donegal,
Fermanagh, Galway, Mayo, Cork, Kerry and Wicklow, where they prefer
plantations of over 25 years of age. There are about 60,000 pairs in Ireland,
which are subject to eruptive movements, triggered off by exhaustion of
food supplies. Many Continental immigrants reach Ireland in the autumn
from September onwards. As none of the 350 Irish ringed siskins have
been recovered to date, we do not know if our birds migrate.

See 'Finches' p.21

ADULT MALE

Redpoll

Carduelis flammea
Deargeadan
COMMON RESIDENT
11.5–14.5 CM

The redpoll is another species whose rapid expansion throughout Ireland is linked to that of coniferous plantations, especially in western areas. Often heard before being seen, it can be identified by its characteristic flight call "teu-teu-teu-tue" and also by a twittering "zee-chee-chee-chee". Adults have a red forehead, a black chin and brown-streaked upper parts. The male has a pink breast and rump in summer. Redpolls are more abundant and widespread than siskins (p.85), with about 70,000 pairs, large numbers of which are found in Cos. Kerry, Clare, Mayo, Donegal and Roscommon. Their favoured nesting habitats are birch woodlands, but as their expansion has shown, they are equally happy amongst the conifers. Whilst birch and alder seeds are their preferred winter food, they are often recorded visiting suburban gardens and bird tables. In the autumn, small flocks of up to 50 birds roam the countryside searching for food, and are very acrobatic while feeding. Large numbers immigrate to Ireland in September/October, including the larger and paler Arctic redpoll and the greyer and less warm-brown Mealy redpoll.

See 'Finches' p.21

JUVENILE

ADULT
FEMALE
SUMMER

ADULT MALE
SUMMER

Crossbill

Loxia curvirostra

Crosghob

RARE RESIDENT. HIGHLY IRRUPTIVE WITH VARIOUS
NUMBER OF VISITORS (LATE JUNE–MID AUGUST)
16.5 CM

ADULT
FEMALE

Crossbills live only in coniferous woodlands, as they are
dependent upon the seeds in the pinecones for their food. After
the cones have been split open by the specially adapted "crossed
bill" they are dropped onto the woodland floor and serve as evidence to
the human observer of the crossbill's presence. Resembling small parrots
with their short tails and bulky heads, crossbills are often seen flying with
a rapid undulating flight in small groups, well above the treetops or heard
calling their distinctive "chip-chip-chip-chi-chi". Males are pinkish-
crimson, with brown wings and a noticeable pink rump. Females have a
yellowish-olive rump and underparts, while both sexes exhibit many colour
variants. Young birds are streaked brown. Large flocks of up to 500 birds
sometimes visit Ireland, following "irruptions" from the Continent brought
about by the exhaustion of pine crops. Many of these birds have stayed
behind to breed. The estimated normal breeding population is upwards of
200 pairs. Crossbills are most abundant in Cos. Wicklow, Kerry, Galway,
Mayo, Down, Armagh, Tyrone, Donegal, Leitrim and Fermanagh, where
they find suitably aged coniferous woodlands.

See 'Finches' p.21

ADULT MALE

Moorland and Uplands

Upland moorland showing signs of erosion. Red grouse will be found in the taller heather while curlew, snipe, meadow pipits, ravens and golden plover will be encountered.

Peat bogs constitute one of the most characteristic features of Ireland, covering about 17 per cent of the land surface. There are two basic types: raised bogs that rise as if they are bread being baked (in some cases, these go up to four metres above the surrounding, flat Midland landscape); and blanket bogs, which occur extensively in western Ireland, both at low level and on hills and mountains. The number of bird species as well as the total number of birds in these habitats are low because of the limited availability of food, which is due to the acidic conditions and the resultant poor biological productivity. In the old days, before the sheep invaded Ireland, the bogs were covered with tall stands of heather that offered much more cover for nesting and, consequently, supported a larger bird population. The commercial exploitation of

Commeragh Mountains, Co. Waterford. Home of peregrine falcon, dipper, ring ouzel and hen harriers.

bogs for fuel has also been detrimental in many instances to birdlife along with the afforestation programmes (the latter, however, providing renewed habitat for certain species).

Skylarks, meadow pipits and snipe are the commonest birds of the bogs and moorlands. Hooded crows and ravens occur, often quartering the bog, inspecting it for carrion or young birds, while mallard visit bog pools to devour the seeds of the floating pondweed. Bogland was once the favoured habitat of the Greenland's white-fronted geese, which came to root up the nutritious stolons of the bog cotton. In recent years though, fewer flocks with smaller numbers have been visiting boglands, the geese preferring the richer, improved grasslands on flat farmland, such as at the Wexford Slobs. Golden plovers are found breeding in mountain bogs in a few, very scattered pairs. Ravens and peregrines breed on many mountain cliffs (while being possibly more numerous in coastal areas), whereas merlins prefer to breed in lowland, blanket bogland. Ring ouzel are present in a few of the mountain areas but only in small numbers. Red grouse continue to decline.

Lowland blanket bogland, Co. Galway, with twelve Bens in distance. Greenland white-fronted geese visit the wilder spots while merlins and herons nest on small wooded islands in the lakes.

Lowland blanket bogland, Co. Mayo. Away from the banks of turf cutting meadow pipits breed, while occassional Greenland whitefronted greese and snipe visit the area.

BIRDS OF PREY

The larger birds of prey are often seen overhead, the wing shape being a useful pointer to identification:

BUZZARD

- large, wings broad and rounded – buzzard (p.67)
- large, wings relatively long for width, held straight – hen harrier (p.93)
- large, wings sharply pointed – peregrine (p.96)

PEREGRINE

Some birds of prey perch during daytime in typical situations:
- on telegraph and similar poles, or fence posts – buzzard and kestrel (p.42)
- on tops and branches of live or dead tree – kestrel
- on garden fences and roofs, and among branches of trees – sparrowhawk (p.66)

SPARROWHAWK

With small birds of prey, flying style is helpful for identification:
- hovering over open ground – kestrel
- flying low and fast over open moorland – merlin (p.95)
- flying low and fast, close to hedges or through woodland – sparrowhawk

KESTREL (HOVERING)

Hen Harrier

Circus cyaneus

Cromán na gcearc

RARE LOCAL RESIDENT. RECENT DECLINE

44–52 CM

ADULT FEMALE

Hen harriers are most likely to be seen quartering the ground in hilly moorland areas – below 500 m and clothed with young forestry plantations, or in coastal regions during winter. The hen harrier has the typical "harrier" flight – low, only a few feet above the ground, and punctuated by leisurely wingbeats followed by long periods of gliding. The wings are held in a shallow "V" form. Males have a striking blue-grey plumage, black wing tips and a large, white rump. The female and juveniles have dark-brown upper parts and broadly streaked underparts. Hen harriers enter spectacular courtship displays involving vertical ascents, close-winged descents and, often, a somersault performed by the male at the top of the climb. When the female is incubating, the male will bring her food and transfer it to her in midflight. Formerly widely distributed throughout Ireland, these harriers became all but extinct by the 1950s; their numbers then picked up dramatically as a result of afforestation – 250–300 breeding pairs were recorded in 1973–75 – but went on to decline as the forests grew taller and unsuitable for them. Today there are only 102 known, plus another 27 suspected breeding pairs in the Republic of Ireland, mostly in the counties of Kerry, Limerick, Cork, Clare, Tipperary and Laois, and a further 31–44 pairs in Northern Ireland, in the counties of Tyrone, Fermanagh and Antrim.

See 'Birds of Prey' p. 92

ADULT MALE

Golden Eagle

Aquila chrysaetos

Iolar fíréan

<small>SCARCE RESIDENT (RE-INTRODUCTION). VAGRANT VISITOR</small>

75–88 CM

ADULT

An extensive breeding bird in the higher mountain ranges of Munster, Connacht and Ulster up to the mid-19th century, it was exterminated by gamekeepers, poisoning and trapping. The last breeding bird recorded in Co. Donegal was in 1910 and in Co. Mayo, 1912. Since then vagrants, almost certainly from Scotland, have been recorded, mostly in Northern Ireland. A pair bred at Fairhead, Co. Antrim, 1953 to 1960, and was observed collecting food (hares) from nearby Mull of Kintyre. In flight they are unmistakable by their large size – 75 per cent longer winged than the buzzard – soaring flight and spread, upcurved primary wing feathers, and a square tail. A five-year re-introduction programme saw the release of six eaglets – brought from Scottish nests – in autumn 2001, at Glenveagh National Park, Co. Donegal. A further eight eaglets were released in 2002, followed by 12 more in 2003. All birds, expect one that died, are now free-flying at Glenveagh and in nearby mountain ranges. First breeding is expected in 2005–06. If the project is successful there could be, in the years to come, 50–100 pairs throughout the country.

See 'Birds of Prey' p. 92

ADULT

Merlin

Falco columbarius

Meirliún

SCARCE RESIDENT. UNCOMMON
PASSAGE MIGRANT AND WINTER VISITOR (MID–
AUGUST TO MAY)
25–30 CM

ADULT FEMALE

The merlin is a very small falcon, usually seen flying low and fast over open ground in pursuit of small birds, especially tender meadow pipits. Its dipping, swerving flight is interspersed with short glides. Once "fixed" on its prey the chase is unrelenting, until the victim is grabbed by the talons. The male has slate-blue upper parts, darkly streaked, rufous underparts and a broad, black terminal band on the tail. The female is larger, with dark brown upper parts. Merlins are also seen perched on low rocks, walls, or fences. They generally nest on the ground, amongst heather in hilly moorlands, but in Northern Ireland they prefer the abandoned nests of hooded crows. In west Galway they breed on densely vegetated island sites in lowland blanket bogs. They also nest in conifer plantations. Their main areas of concentration are the Wicklow uplands, the western counties of Galway, Mayo and Donegal, and also Northern Ireland. In winter they move to lower, often coastal, areas. The estimated Irish breeding population is 110–130 pairs. Irish merlins generally remain within 50 km of their natal area, while birds from Iceland and other northern countries winter in Ireland.

See 'Birds of Prey' p.92

ADULT MALE

Peregrine

Falco peregrinus

Fabhcún gorm

SCARCE RESIDENT, RECENT INCREASE

36–48 CM

JUVENILE

The peregrine is a compactly built falcon with long, sharply pointed wings, a slightly tapering tail and a fast, pigeon-like dashing flight, making it look like a flying cigar. The male has blue-grey upper parts and buffish, white underparts. The female is larger and browner. Both share a very pronounced moustachial stripe. Their preferred habitats are inland cliff sites, but they have now become almost as frequent on coastal cliffs and particularly on the western islands. When disturbed at their nesting site they can be quite noisy, persistently calling "kek-kek-kek-kek", while one or both of the birds fly around in an agitated manner, involving rapid wingbeats interspersed by gliding. Peregrines pair for life and return to their former nest site year after year. Forty years ago there was a severe population reduction in Ireland and Britain due to organochlorine insecticides – followed by a remarkable recovery as the harmful pesticides were withdrawn. Now there are about 500 breeding pairs scattered widely throughout Ireland. Outside the breeding season, they are most likely encountered in coastal areas.

See 'Birds of Prey' p.92

ADULT MALE

Red Grouse

Lagopus lagopus hibernicus

Cearc fhraoigh

LOCAL RESIDENT, DECLINING

37–42 CM

ADULT

FEMALE

Red grouse are perhaps the most characteristic birds of heather moorland. They are likely to be encountered when disturbed by dogs, or walking. They fly low after an explosive take-off and alternate rapid wingbeats with long glides. Sometimes they are solitary, but they also occur in small packs. Red grouse are rufous brown and look almost black from a distance. They have white, feathered legs and a red wattle above each eye. The Irish red grouse has a yellower summer plumage and is whiter in winter, and is therefore regarded by some authorities as distinct from the British species. During the breeding season, the cock calls a loud, barking "go-bak-go-bak-bak-bak-bak". Thinly scattered, these grouse occur in the counties of Wicklow, Kerry, Cork, Donegal, Mayo and Sligo, and in Northern Ireland. There has been a substantial decline in numbers since the 1920s as a result of the break-up of sporting estates and lack of moorland management. An estimated 500–2,000 pairs bred in Ireland in 2003.

ADULT MALE

CHATS

Wheatear (p.181), whinchat (p.99) and stonechat (p.100)
- rather robin-like birds, which stand or perch fairly upright
- frequently flick their tails
- feed mainly on the ground, on insects
- give various "chak" or "tik" calls
- usually sing from a prominent perch, or in flight
- favour rough, open ground with gorse or other bushes (stonechat and whinchat), or stony heath and moorland (wheatear)
- show white/whitish on rump and/or tail in flight; amount and position are important for identification
- sexes differ markedly in wheatear and stonechat, but not in whinchat
- head patterns are distinctive, especially in males

FEMALE WHINCHAT

FEMALE STONECHAT

FEMALE WHEATEAR

Whinchat

Saxicola rubetra

Caislín aitinn

LOCAL SUMMER VISITOR

MAY–OCTOBER

12.5 CM

ADULT
FEMALE

The whinchat is a summer visitor, in contrast to the stonechat (p.100) which is an all-year resident. The two are easily confused, as both are small, with streaky brown upper parts and warm buff throats and chests. Both like perching on the tops of small bushes, flitting from one to another. The diagnostic feature distinguishing the whinchat from the stonechat is the prominent white eyestripe, though somewhat duller in the female whinchat. Their scolding call is a sharp "tic-tic" and their song, delivered from a bush top or from the air, is a short warbling similar to the stonechat's. The whinchat is more frequently encountered in the rough agricultural landscape of the Midlands, whereas the stonechat is more likely to be seen in coastal areas, as well as in hilly moorland and on rough hillsides. The whinchat is less frequent on upland pastures and hillsides. Whinchats are most widespread in the counties of Antrim, Donegal, Roscommon, Westmeath, Wicklow and Kildare, though these birds also breed in many other counties. There are an estimated 1,250–2,500 breeding pairs in Ireland.

See 'Chats' p.98

ADULT MALE

Stonechat

Saxicola torquata

Caislín cloch

FAIRLY COMMON RESIDENT

12.5 CM

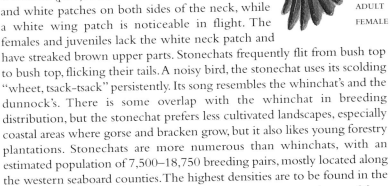

ADULT FEMALE

The stonechat is rounder and plumper than the whinchat (p.99). The male has a distinct black head and white patches on both sides of the neck, while a white wing patch is noticeable in flight. The females and juveniles lack the white neck patch and have streaked brown upper parts. Stonechats frequently flit from bush top to bush top, flicking their tails. A noisy bird, the stonechat uses its scolding "wheet, tsack–tsack" persistently. Its song resembles the whinchat's and the dunnock's. There is some overlap with the whinchat in breeding distribution, but the stonechat prefers less cultivated landscapes, especially coastal areas where gorse and bracken grow, but it also likes young forestry plantations. Stonechats are more numerous than whinchats, with an estimated population of 7,500–18,750 breeding pairs, mostly located along the western seaboard counties. The highest densities are to be found in the counties of Cork, Kerry, Limerick, Clare, Connemara, north-west Mayo and south-west Donegal. The upland birds move down to the coast in the autumn and a few migrate south to Spain.

See 'Chats' p.98

ADULT MALE

Ring Ouzel

Turdus torquatus

Lon creige

RARE LOCAL SUMMER VISITOR, (APRIL–SEPTEMBER) DECLINING
SCARCE PASSAGE MIGRANT (APRIL–OCTOBER)
23–24 CM

During the breeding season, this sooty, black-plumaged thrush with a white crescent on the chest is found in a few upland areas. When folded, the wings have a pale patch. Females are browner, with a less pronounced white crescent. Juveniles resemble a young brown blackbird and have no crescent. Much shyer and more difficult to approach than the blackbird, their alarm call is a piping "tac-tac-tac". They often nest on a rocky outcrop or ledge near streams or in ravines. They were formerly more common in Ireland, nesting in most counties up to the turn of the century. A decline set in for the next 50 years as numbers and distribution shrank. They are now found in mountainous areas in the counties of Cork and Kerry; in the Mourne Mountains, Co. Down; in the north and west of county Donegal (only 15 pairs found in 2002); in the Wicklow uplands and in south Connemara. About 30–50 pairs breed in Ireland (2002). The first migrants arrive at the end of March or beginning of April, and return in October to their Mediterranean and north-west African wintering grounds.

See 'Thrushes' p.56

JUVENILE

ADULT MALE

Raven

Corvus corax

Fiach dubh

<small>COMMON RESIDENT, RECENT INCREASE</small>

64 CM

The raven is distinguished from other crows by its large size and wedge-shaped tail in flight. Its other features are a glossy black plumage, a massive bill and straggly throat feathers. Ravens can be remarkably acrobatic in flight, particularly during courtship, tumbling, rolling over and even flying upside down for short periods. The usual flight note is a deep, croaking "pruk-pruk-pruk". Of the Irish breeding birds, ravens are amongst the earliest, starting in February, and can become extremely anguished and aggressive if their nest is approached too closely.

ADULT

They often peck the ground violently as a substitute for attacking the intruder. Ravens pair for life and in the autumn/winter often gather at places where sheep carrion is available. They nest widely throughout Ireland, with at least 3,500 pairs, settling mostly on coastal cliffs, upland cliffs, in old quarries and in trees. Young birds disperse widely after fledging, while some winter visitors come from Scotland.

ADULT

Linnet

Carduelis cannabina

Gleoiseach

COMMON RESIDENT

13.5 CM

ADULT FEMALE

Linnets are noisy, restless finches whose twittering, attractive song made them a popular cage bird in the 19th century. In summer the male has a crimson crown and breast, and a chestnut back. The tail is forked, with white sides to it. Females lack the crimson and are generally drabber. Linnets are gregarious from autumn to spring, when small flocks roam the countryside in search of weed seeds, mostly picked off the ground. Their song is best described as a rapid and excited twittering without a fixed structure. Their favourite habitat during the breeding season is rough, uncultivated farmland with scrub cover. Young forestry plantations are also important breeding areas. With a population of about 130,000 pairs, the linnet is a widespread bird occurring in all counties as well as on many marine islands. During the winter, linnets prefer open agricultural countryside as dictated by their weed-seed diet, and concentrate in the south and eastern parts of the country, though never too far from the coast. Large numbers of passage birds have been recorded at bird observatories in Donegal, Wexford and Cork. They were possibly en route to western France, Spain or Portugal. Some Irish birds travel south to the Continent.

See 'Finches' p.21

ADULT MALE SUMMER

Freshwater: rivers, lakes and marshes

Blessington Reservoir, Co. Wicklow. Good for teal, mallard, coot, moorhen, great crested grebes and 'hawking' swallows and sand martins. Greylag geese in fields at edge of water. (Photo Redmond Cabot)

The famous Irish naturalist Robert Lloyd Praeger encapsulated thus: "Ireland is essentially a land of lakes – from Lough Neagh, the largest sheet of fresh water in the British Isles, down to hundreds of lowland meres and mountain tarns." All this water provides very rich habitats both for the resident breeding birds and the visiting waterfowl from the Arctic north. Yet, what is good for wildlife is not always appreciated by farmers, many of whom face a constant struggle to overcome flooded lands.

Most large lakes are set on the soft limestone rocks in the central plain of Ireland. They are shallow and biologically productive, with extensive marginal vegetation, good fish populations, several kinds of insects and freshwater invertebrates, and this, in turn, supports a rich and varied birdlife. The best examples of these types of lakes are Loughs Sheelin, Co. Cavan; Ennell, Co. Westmeath;

Derravaragh, Co. Westmeath; Corrib, Co. Galway; Conn, Co. Mayo; Mask, Co. Mayo; Ree, Co. Longford; Derg, Co. Tipperary; Gill, Co. Kerry; Key, Co. Roscommon and the lower lakes of Killarney, Co. Kerry.

Spending most of their lives on these lakes are the little grebe, the great-crested grebe, the coot, mute swans, tufted ducks and moorhens. Other birds regularly visit them for feeding purposes, such as the heron, the kingfisher and the cormorant, but also the swallow, the sand martin and the swift hawking for insects above the water. Some gulls and terns breed on islands, especially in western lakes, such as the black-headed

Lake, river and drumlin landscape. Whooper swans frequent the lakes and feed along river margins in winter. Tufted duck and pochard are common in lakes.

gull, common gull, lesser black-backed gull and common tern. The redshank and common sandpiper are found breeding along many of the rocky and marshy shorelines of these great lakes.

However, not all lakes boast abundant bird life. Those set on hard rocks, such as granite with acid waters, do not permit the growth of a diverse and luxuriant vegetation; they support many fewer invertebrates and as a result, accommodate only a limited range of birds. They are

Rocky streams are ideal habitats for grey wagtails and dippers.

found in Connemara, Co. Donegal, west Mayo, parts of counties Cork, Kerry and Wicklow and parts of Co. Down. Standing on their shores, one could expect to see the occasional red-breasted merganser, common sandpiper or perhaps the red-throated diver, which breeds in only one or two locations in Co. Donegal. Because a good number of these lakes are remote and free from human disturbance, they are attractive to the sensitive and shy Greenland white-fronted geese, which visit them to roost, drink and preen.

Rivers in lowland areas are slow-moving and rich in food ranging from aquatic insects to minnows, trout, salmon and floating weeds. In the reedy backwaters of these rivers, mute swans, mallard, moorhens and little grebes breed, while kingfishers nest in sandy riverbanks. Turbulent and rocky streams play host to different insect populations: their larvae, found under stones along the stream bottom, make up the dipper's diet; the grey wagtail hops from stone to stone, eagerly snapping up the newly-hatched and other flying insects.

Many marshes and reed beds envelop the Midland and other lakes. These are essential habitats for many birds, as they provide good nesting cover as well as general protection from predators. Damp, marshy meadows along rivers and lakes accommodate the snipe; breeding reed buntings and sedge warblers occupy the tall reed beds, along with the teal and the rarely seen water rail that squeals like a piglet. In the autumn, swallows, pied wagtails, sand martins, starlings and sedge warblers often roost in the reed beds.

Turloughs, or temporary lakes, are a special feature of the Irish landscape and of immense importance to waterfowl populations. They occur in low-lying areas, principally in the limestone regions of counties Mayo, Galway, Roscommon and Clare. Connected to the underground water table by a swallow hole, they fill up in wet weather from October until April, and recede as the water table drops again during the summer. The vegetation in turloughs benefits greatly from the fluctuating water level: in winter, the water acts as an insulating blanket, protecting the grass from the frost; in summer, the nutrients of bird droppings, deposited during the winter and spring, ensure a prolific growth of the grass sward. Turloughs host a variety of birds, such as the wintering golden plover, wigeon, shoveler, teal, lapwing, dunlin, whooper and Bewick's swans, Greenland white-fronted geese and many other waterfowl.

Many of these temporary lakes have been destroyed through arterial drainage, but there are some that still survive. Throughout the country in the mid-1990s, there were 61 undrained turloughs exceeding 10

Booterstown Marsh, Dun Laoghaire, Co. Dublin. A brackish waterbody where snipe, teal, mallard, lapwing, coot, moorhen and many waders can be watched from the main road. (Photo: Redmond Cabot)

hectares, with a total area of some 31,000 hectares. The most important remaining one for birds is Rahasane Turlough, west of Craughwell, Co. Galway. Similar to the turloughs and equally attractive to wintering wildfowl are the flooded grasslands of the rivers Shannon, Little Brosna, Co. Offaly; Suck, Co. Roscommon; and Blackwater, Co. Waterford. The Shannon callow lands are very important breeding sites, albeit for the declining populations of curlew, lapwing, snipe and redshank, as well as for corncrakes. Two of Ireland's rarest breeding species, the shoveler and black-tailed godwit, also breed there in small numbers.

Rahasane Turlough, Co. Galway. Ireland's premier wetland, where thousands of ducks, swans and waders can be seen during the winter when water levels are low.

GREBES

Great crested (p.112) and little (opposite) grebes
• are water birds with sharply-pointed bills and a 'tailless'
appearance
• sexes look alike
• surface dive, sliding under or
jump-diving
• fly less often than ducks
• breed on freshwater loughs; some
winter on coastal inshore waters
• build floating nests attached to emergent vegetation
• chicks have striped heads and necks, and are often carried on
their parent's back
• size (great crested), pattern and
colour of head and neck,
and shape of body (little), are
main distinguishing features

NESTLING GREAT
CRESTED GREBE

NESTLING LITTLE GREBE

LITTLE GREBE
ADULT WINTER

GREAT CRESTED GREBE
ADULT WINTER

Little Grebe (or Dabchick)

Tachybaptus ruficollis

Spágaire tonn

FAIRLY COMMON RESIDENT

25–29 CM

The little grebe is the smallest of our grebes and has a blunt-ended appearance with a short neck. In summer, the grebe has dark brown upper parts with chestnut cheeks and throat. The base of the white-tipped black bill is yellow-green, as is the gape. In winter, the upper parts are paler and the chestnut cheeks change to a buffish white colour. Little grebes are shy and skulking, and can be easily missed or overlooked. Small lakes, ponds and waterways, with plenty of vegetation to provide cover and suitable anchorage for their floating nests, are favourite habitats. During spring, the grebes have a mad-sounding, whinnying trill which is made by both birds during courtship. They dive either silently or with a small leap and splash, remaining submerged for about 15 seconds while hunting sticklebacks, other small fish and insects. The grebe is a widespread breeder, with 3,000–6,000 pairs well distributed throughout the country. After breeding, some little grebes move to coastal lagoons and estuaries, while others remain in, or close to, their breeding areas.

See 'Grebes' p. 110

ADULT SUMMER

ADULT
WINTER

Great Crested Grebe

Podiceps cristatus

Foitheach mór

<small>FAIRLY COMMON RESIDENT, INCREASING</small>

46–51 CM

The great crested grebe is our largest grebe, with a conspicuous black, double-horned head crest and ear tufts of black-tipped, extended chestnut frills. The bill is long and the neck is slender, long and silky-white in colour. During the nineteenth century, the grebe was brought close to extinction in Britain (only 42 pairs remained) by a fashion demand for grebe feathers to decorate women's hats. The ear tufts and horned crest are moulted and lost in the autumn. The courtship ceremonies are a remarkable sight as the birds shake their heads while the ear tufts are erected. They perform a "penguin dance", in which both birds dive, bring up weed, tread on the water and come breast to breast. There are an estimated 4,150 individuals that breed on large shallow lakes fringed with reed beds. The bulk of the population is located north of a line, from Limerick-Dundalk, and the numbers are increasing. After the breeding season, some birds move to coastal regions, while others remain in their breeding areas. Several authorities state that there is an influx of west European great crested grebes during the winter.

See 'Grebes' p.110

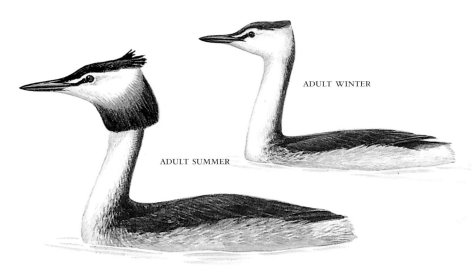

ADULT WINTER

ADULT SUMMER

Grey Heron

Ardea cinerea

Corr reísc

COMMON RESIDENT

90–98 CM

Often called a crane by country people, the heron is unmistakable with its long yellow bill, long narrow legs, a long neck and a grey and white body. When standing tall in shallow water, patiently waiting to stab a fish, or standing hunched up on a riverbank or in flight with its broad wings, its neck retracted and its long dangling legs, the heron cannot be confused with any other bird. Its call is a gruff harsh "frank", often delivered in flight when mobbed by gulls and crows disturbed by its predator-like appearance. The heron is widely distributed as a breeding bird, with about 3,650 pairs scattered in small colonies, generally less than 50 nests. Its nesting habitats range from the small islets in Connemara bogland to cliffs and treetops in woodland sites. After breeding, herons disperse locally to coastal areas, marshes, rivers and lakes, seldom travelling more than 30km from their natal grounds. A few birds are known to have moved outside Ireland, to Scotland (6), England (3) and Wales (2). Scottish, English and Continental herons visit Ireland in the autumn and winter.

ADULT

ADULT

Mute Swan

Cygnus olor
Eala bhalbh
VERY COMMON RESIDENT
145–160 CM

The mute swan differs from the whooper (opposite) and Bewick's (p.116) swan by having an orange bill with a black base and large forehead knob, which is much smaller in the female. The neck is held in a crooked S form. When flying, the wing beats make a distinctive and waxy singing noise. Contrary to its name, it is not mute, and makes loud hissing and explosive snorting sounds, especially if annoyed at the nest. During the breeding season, the pairs keep to themselves, often being very aggressive to other nearby swans. The birds are sociable outside the breeding season, when large numbers may gather together. They feed by dipping their necks under the water, but also by "up-ending" like ducks in order to pluck deeper vegetation. Although the history of the Irish mute swans is not fully known, they are thought to have been brought in by English landlords as ornamental species to adorn their private lakes and ponds. Originally wild, mute swans were domesticated during the 12th century in Britain, and were the property of the Crown until the 18th century, when the supervision of the King's Swan Master was lifted and they reverted to the wild. About 20,000 birds are widely scattered throughout the country.

JUVENILE

MALE

Whooper Swan

Cygnus cygnus

Eala ghlórach

WINTER VISITOR (OCTOBER–APRIL).

VERY RARE BREEDER

145–160 CM

The whooper swan is distinguished from the mute swan (opposite) by its bill, which is yellow with a black tip and has no knob at the base. Also, while sitting on water, the neck is held stiffly upright. When flying, the wings do not make a singing sound and when on water, the body of the whooper swan is longer and more slender than that of the mute swan. The tail of the whooper is usually held parallel to the water surface, while that of the mute swan is often at an angle of 45°. Whooper swans have a characteristic call when flying or on water, which is a bugle-like double note "whoop-a". As with all other swans and geese, the family party remains together after the breeding season and throughout the winter before returning to Iceland. Juveniles are easily picked out in the winter flocks by their uniform, grey plumage and flesh-coloured bills. On arrival in Ireland in October, the birds exhibit much excitement as they land on lakes with noisy wing flapping, neck pumping and vigorous calling. In January 2000, 12,730 birds were counted in Ireland at 414 sites – turloughs, shallow lakes and river callows – with an increasing tendency to graze on reseeded grassland. The juveniles loaf near the breeding grounds for one or two summers before they start breeding. One or two pairs breed in Ireland intermittently.

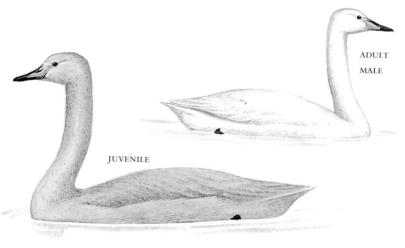

ADULT
MALE

JUVENILE

Bewick's Swan

Cygnus columbianus bewickii

Eala Bewick

WINTER VISITOR (OCTOBER–APRIL)

115–127 CM

The Bewick's swan is noticeably smaller and daintier than the whooper (p.115) and mute (p.114) swan, with a shorter neck and smaller bill. Also, the Bewick's swan has a black bill with a yellow base, as opposed to the yellow bill with a black tip of the whooper. Young birds are pale grey, like immature whooper swans. The Bewick's swan's call notes are similar to the whooper's but more highly pitched and more musical and cackling. To add to the confusion (Bewick's swans were only distinguished from the whooper in 1824), they put on the same kind of triumphant display on arriving in Ireland as the whooper. In January 2000, only 382 wintering birds were counted in Ireland, scattered in small flocks throughout the country on lakes, turloughs – particularly in counties Clare, Galway and Roscommon – on rivers and on adjacent callow lands, and more recently on improved agricultural land, where they forage on waste root crops such as sugar beet, potatoes, grain stubble and winter cereals. The largest concentrations of Bewick's swans are found in Co. Wexford; Loughs Neagh and Beg, Co. Antrim; the River Shannon and the associated callow lands. During hard weather conditions in Europe, large numbers move west into Ireland. The Irish wintering birds breed in western Siberia.

ADULT

JUVENILE

Greenland White-fronted Goose

Anser albifrons flavirostris

Gé bhánéadanach

LOCAL WINTER VISITOR (SEPT–APRIL)

65–78 CM

This goose belongs to the "grey goose" group, and is smaller and darker than the greylag (p.118). Adults have a prominent white forehead, extending to the base of the orange-yellow bill, and broad black barring on the breast. Juveniles lack the white forehead and chest markings. This is "the" goose of Ireland, as approximately half of the world's population of 27,000 birds winters in this country, while the others winter in Scotland, mainly on the island of Islay. Greenland white-fronts are widely scattered throughout Ireland on western blanket bogs, marshy wet callow lands, Midland raised bogs and on improved agricultural land. Their largest haunt is on the Wexford Slobs, where about 7,000 spend the winter. Their haunting, shrieking, clamouring call in flight enables identification at long range as they come flying high overhead, in V formation. They are remarkably agile in flight and have the incredible ability to leap up and take off almost vertically. If frightened when landing, they can "reverse engines" and shoot up perpendicularly. Numbers declined during the 1960s and 1970s, but showed a healthy increase to 35,500 in 1990, responding to a hunting moratorium in 1982. However, numbers declined mysteriously and in spring 2002, only 26,422 were counted during the international census.

See 'Geese' p.120

ADULT

Greylag Goose

Anser anser

Gé ghlas

SCARCE LOCAL FERAL RESIDENT, INCREASING.

LOCAL WINTER VISITOR (OCTOBER–APRIL)

75–90 CM

The greylag is somewhat similar to the Greenland white-fronted goose (p.117), but larger and differentiated by striking, pale grey forewings, which are very noticeable in flight. The head is much larger, with a big bright orange bill. The legs are flesh-coloured, while the overall appearance of the goose is a uniform grey-brown. The flight call is quite different from the white-front's and is a deep sonorous "aahng-ung-ung", somewhat similar to the typical farmyard goose, which is a descendant of the wild greylag. It is thought that the greylag bred as a wild species in the Bog of Allen and in Co. Down during the 18th century. Greylag geese, which winter in Ireland, are from the Icelandic breeding stock, most of which winter in Scotland. Once very numerous, with over 6,000 wintering on the Wexford Slobs, numbers declined throughout Ireland to about 750 in 1967. Since 1975, the population of wintering birds has been increasing and totalled about 8,000 in 1998–1999. Some large flocks of 1,000 are sometimes seen. The major haunts of the greylag are Lough Swilly, Co Donegal; Stabannon, Co. Louth; Poulaphouca Reservoir, Co. Wicklow; Coolfin, Co. Waterford and Lambay Island, Co. Dublin. There is a thriving feral population of some 977 birds, counted at 30 sites in 1994.

See 'Geese' p.120

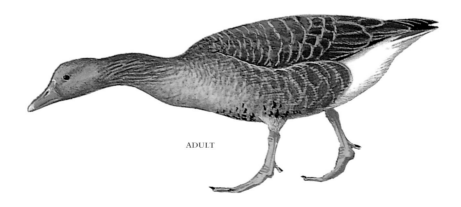

ADULT

Canada Goose

Branta canadensis

Gé Cheanadach

LOCAL FERAL RESIDENT, INCREASING

RARE GENUINE VAGRANT (OCTOBER–APRIL)

90–100 CM

This is a large dark goose which superficially resembles the much smaller barnacle goose (p.154), but its upper parts are brown and the black neck does not extend to the breast, while a very distinctive, broad white patch covers only the throat. Canada geese are noisy birds, frequently calling "aa-honk" on the wing and sometimes on the ground. A few genuinely wild and smaller varieties visit Ireland from Canada, often accompanying Greenland white-fronts during the winter, and can sometimes be seen on the Wexford Slobs. Our large and resident Canada geese are descendants of feral birds, probably brought over from English collections during the 19th century to adorn the ponds of private estates in Cos. Antrim, Down and Dublin. In 1970, thirteen small collections were recorded in Ireland. Today, about 1,000 feral breeding birds are increasing, with concentrations in Strangford Lough, Co. Down, where they have spread to other nearby lakes. They are also found in lower Lough Erne, Co. Fermanagh, where they are quickly colonising water areas in the nearby counties Cavan and Leitrim. Other birds are reported from Lough Swilly and Ardara in Co. Donegal, while those breeding at the Lough in Cork city are spreading out to the marshes of nearby Ballycotton, Co. Cork.

See 'Geese' p.120

ADULT

GEESE

Greenland white-fronted (p.117), greylag (p.118), barnacle (p.154), Canada (p.119), light-bellied brent (p.187) and pink-footed (p.186) geese
- are mainly winter visitors
- usually feed on fields, marshes, bogs and in estuaries by day and roost on water or moorland at night
- are very gregarious and feed in close flocks
- often fly in wavering lines or V formation
- always have some alert 'lookouts' when feeding
- differ in pattern and/or colour of head and neck, size and colour of bill, and colour of legs
- some have distinctive wing colours (visible in flight) or breast markings
- all show white on rump/tail in flight
- with experience, can often be identified by their calls

DUCKS

Ducks
- often have markedly different breeding plumages in male and female
- during summer, moult males (in eclipse) lose distinctive colouring and look very like females
- often have distinctive white or coloured bars or patches on their wings
- have differently-shaped bills according to the foods they take
- are often separated into groups according to how and/or where they feed:

Surface feeding ducks: mallard (p.124), teal (p.123), wigeon (p.190), pintail (p.191), gadwall (p.122) and shoveler (p.125)
- dabble in shallow water or up-end
- feed mainly on vegetable matter
- spring into flight from the water

MALLARD

- often have a blue or green bar (speculum) at the back of the wing
- often rest, and sometimes feed, on land

Diving ducks: tufted (p.128), goldeneye (p.126), pochard (p.127) and scaup (p.189)

TUFTED DUCK

- dive for food, often with a jump before going under
- feed mainly on small water animals
- usually patter along the surface when taking off
- often have conspicuous white wing bars or patches
- come ashore only to nest
- can be confused with grebes (p.112), coot (p.131) or moorhen (p.129)

Saw-billed ducks: red-breasted merganser (p.158)
- dive for food, often sliding under head first
- feed exclusively on fish
- have long bodies and very long slim bills

RED–BREASTED
MERGANSER

- sometimes rest on rocks or logs but stay close to water
- can be confused with divers (p.146)

Sea ducks: eider (p.156), common scoter (p.155) and long-tailed duck (p.157)
- dive for food
- feed on shellfish and crustaceans
- apart from eider, are unlikely to be seen ashore

EIDER

Shelduck (p.188)

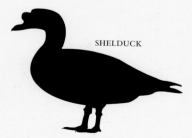

SHELDUCK

- is almost goose-sized
- feeds over mudflats
- occurs only locally inland

Gadwall

Anas strepera

Gadual

RARE LOCAL RESIDENT

UNCOMMON WINTER VISITOR (OCTOBER–APRIL)

46–56 CM

At a distance, the gadwall has the general shape of its close relative, the mallard (p.124), but is smaller. It also has a drab, greyish appearance. Up close, a fine salt-and-pepper speckled pattern can be seen on the head and neck. The bill is grey, the back and flanks have a delicate vermiculated pattern, while a pronounced black "stern" contrasts with the grey plumage. The female is mottled brown like the female mallard. Both sexes have a white wing speculum which is very conspicuous in flight and is a diagnostic feature. Sometimes, a small patch of the speculum can be seen when the birds are sitting on water. Gadwall are shy and not very vocal birds, often found wintering with mallard. There is a small and increasing breeding population of 30-50 pairs, concentrated in Lough Neagh, Co. Antrim and in counties Wexford, Galway, Cork and Down. There are at least 700–800 wintering birds scattered throughout the country, mostly in shallow freshwater lakes. The largest numbers are to be found on the Corofin Lakes and Ballyallia Lake, Co. Clare; at Tacumshin and Lady's Island Lake, Co. Wexford and Lough Carra, Co. Mayo. Most Irish wintering birds come from Iceland, with other birds from Scotland, England, Germany, Denmark and the Netherlands.

See 'Ducks' p.120–1

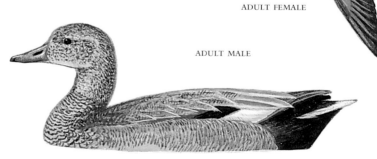

ADULT FEMALE

ADULT MALE

Teal

Anas crecca

Praslacha

UNCOMMON RESIDENT, DECLINING

COMMON WINTER VISITOR (SEPT–MARCH)

34–38 CM

The teal is our smallest duck and its size distinguishes it from all other ducks. At a distance, the male looks grey with a dark head. Creamy white patches on either side of a black "stern" are very conspicuous. Up close, the head is chestnut with an extended dark green eye-band. The female is speckled brown and both sexes have a bright green wing speculum. During winter, the constant and musical "krit-krit" contact call of the males is a feature of small and large flocks. Being shy and somewhat secretive, they tend to lurk in, or close to, the vegetated margins of lakes and ponds. Sitting on the water like neat corks, they can spring up from the surface when disturbed and are extremely agile on the wing, flying in compact flocks, wheeling and swirling in unison like waders. Numbers breeding in Ireland appear to be declining, with only about 350–550 pairs in 2002. Breeders favour small moorland pools and small lakes with good vegetation cover. Most birds are located north-west of a line, running from Limerick to Dundalk. During the winter, large numbers of Continental birds come into Ireland to swell the population to about 50,000.

See 'Ducks' p.120–1

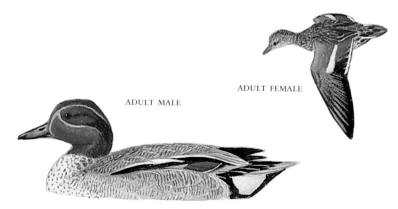

ADULT FEMALE

ADULT MALE

Mallard

Anas platyrhynchos
Lacha fhiáin
VERY COMMON RESIDENT
WINTER VISITOR (SEPT–APRIL)
50–65 CM

ADULT FEMALE

The mallard is Ireland's most ubiquitous and possibly best-known waterfowl. The drake has a stunning dark green glossy head, a white collar and a purple-brown breast. The female is mottled brown with a dark olive bill. Both have a purple speculum (wing patch) boarded by black and white. Their legs are orange. During the eclipse plumage period (July-September), males moult their bright feathers and, for a while, have an appearance similar to the female. Males frequently "up-end" for food, while the females tend to dabble. Many have adapted to a semi-domesticated existence, living on park ponds and on canals in urban areas, feeding on handouts from man. Many mallards have jumbled-up genetics as a result of accidental cross-breeding with farm ducks and other impure individuals, which may have been introduced into the wild population through game club restocking programmes. Birds breeding on remote western islands are probably the closest to genuine wild mallard. Mallard are widespread throughout the country, with about 23,000 breeding pairs. In the autumn, considerable numbers of immigrants come from Britain, along with lesser numbers from the Continent. Large gatherings occur on lakes in August and September after the breeding season.

See 'Ducks' p. 120–1

ADULT MALE

Shoveler

Anas clypeata
Spadalach
SCARCE LOCAL RESIDENT
WINTER VISITOR (AUGUST–APRIL)
44–52 CM

The shoveler has an enormous spatulate bill, which is disproportionately large in comparison with its body size. The male is a brightly contrasted bird with a dark green head and white breast. The flanks and belly are chestnut. As with many other ducks, the female is brownish. Both sexes have a pale blue forewing, which is conspicuous in flight. On the water, they sit low and are generally quiet. When feeding, the spatulate bill is used continuously to dabble in water, filtering out small animals and vegetation. Shovelers are rare breeding birds, with about 70–100 pairs concentrated in Lough Neagh, Co. Antrim and in the Shannon river callows, with other pairs in suitable lowland habitats (2002). There is a large influx of shovelers from Scandinavia, Russia and Iceland, as well as some from Scotland and northern England in winter, when about 4,000 birds are scattered in small flocks mostly in the Midlands and the west. However, quite large numbers can be seen in several east coast estuaries, such as Rogerstown, Co. Dublin and at North Bull Island, Dublin or on Lough Owel and nearby Lough Iron, Co. Westmeath at the beginning of the winter.

See 'Ducks' p. 120–1

ADULT
FEMALE

ADULT MALE

Goldeneye

Bucephala clangula

Órshúileach

Winter visitor (October–March)

42–50 CM

The goldeneye is superficially similar to the drake tufted duck (p.128), but is more compact and smaller, with a white chest and a characteristic circular white patch between the eye and the bill which is visible from a considerable distance. The head is triangular in shape and the bill is short. The female goldeneye has mottled grey upper parts and a chocolate-brown head without the white spot, but has a white collar. Both sexes have prominent white wing patches extending almost to the leading edge of the wing. Goldeneye are winter visitors from Sweden, Finland, Norway and Russia. They generally arrive from October onwards, estuaries and coastal loughs being their favoured wintering habitats. However, many occur in small flocks in Midland lakes. About 11,000 birds winter in Ireland, with most (up to 8,500) on Lough Neagh, Co. Antrim. Spending most of their time diving, goldeneye are much more restless than tufted ducks and pochards, with which they often associate. Birds have been seen in Ireland during summer, and one pair bred at Lough Neagh in 2000 following the remarkable increase in the Scottish population since special nesting boxes were set up in the early 1970s. It is probably only a matter of time before others breed.

See 'Ducks' p. 120–1

ADULT FEMALE

ADULT MALE

Pochard

Aythya ferina

Póiseard

RARE LOCAL RESIDENT

COMMON WINTER VISITOR (AUGUST–MARCH)

42–49 CM

The male pochard has a chestnut-red head and neck, a grey back and flanks, a black breast and black tail. The drake cannot be confused with any other common diving duck in Ireland. Females, however, are a dull brown and can be mistaken for the female tufted duck (p.128), with which they commonly associate. However, the pochard has a bluish ring around the tip of the bill and a blue area at the base of the bill. In flight, the wing band is grey, and not white as in the tufted duck. Pochards spend much of their time sitting heavily on the water, seemingly immobile and loafing around in the centre of small loughs or larger lakes. When diving, they either give a small jump or sometimes they just slip under the water. They are scarce but increasing as breeders in Ireland, with probably 30-50 pairs, mostly confined to Lough Neagh, Co. Antrim and Cos. Roscommon, Galway and Cork. Large numbers of up to 40,000 birds from northern and western Europe winter in Ireland and can be seen on many freshwater lakes. Very large concentrations occur on Lough Corrib, Co. Galway (12,000) and Lough Derravaragh, Co. Westmeath (3,400) in early autumn.

See 'Ducks' p.120–1

ADULT
FEMALE

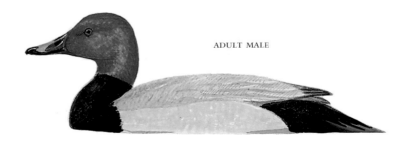

ADULT MALE

Tufted Duck

Aythya fuligula
Lacha bhadánach
LOCAL RESIDENT
COMMON WINTER VISITOR (AUGUST–MARCH)
40–47 CM

The drake tufted duck has a striking black and white plumage during the breeding season, with a thin drooping crest which is normally apparent. When the males moult and go into eclipse plumage (July-September), they resemble their dark brown female counterparts. In flight, both sexes have a broad white wing bar, extending the length of the wing, a feature which helps to distinguish tufted ducks from other similar species. Their habits are similar to those of the pochard (p.127), but they seem to be more active and less "heavy" on water. They dive for their vegetable and animal food in shallower waters than used by pochard. There are about 2,000 breeding pairs nesting in rush and reed-fringed lakes, with most birds located north of a line, between Limerick and Dundalk. The largest breeding concentrations are found in the biggest lakes – Loughs Neagh, Co. Antrim; Corrib, Mask and Conn, Co. Mayo; Ree, Co. Roscommon and Derg, Co. Clare. Little is known about the movements or migration of Irish-bred birds. Up to 40,000 birds from Iceland, Scandinavia, the Baltic states, Scotland and the Netherlands spend the winter in Ireland (mostly on Lough Neagh – 20,000), forming mixed flocks with pochards.

See 'Ducks' p.120–1

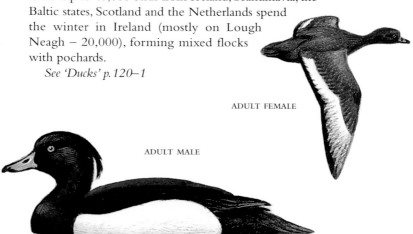

ADULT FEMALE

ADULT MALE

Moorhen

Gallinula chloropus

Cearc uisce

VERY COMMON RESIDENT

32–35 CM

ADULT

The moorhen is a brownish-black plumaged water bird with red on its forehead extending onto its yellow bill. The white undertail coverts are noticeable, as the tail is flicked constantly when the bird is swimming or walking on land. The moorhen is a perky, nervous bird, scurrying off into the vegetation when disturbed. When moving through water, its head jerks backwards and forward in a somewhat comical manner. It mostly picks its predominantly vegetable food off the water surface, but will occasionally dive under water. Its contact call is a harsh "kittick" and its flight is low with its green legs dangling behind the tail. Moorhens occur on most small or large ponds, in slow-moving rivers, marshes and ornamental park ponds, where they require marginal vegetation for shelter and nesting. There are an estimated 75,000 pairs in Ireland, the birds only being absent from upland hilly areas. Some moorhens move after the breeding season, but stay within about 20 km of their breeding areas. Irish moorhens do not migrate. However, some north-west European birds from Sweden, Denmark and the Netherlands, as well as some from Scotland, spend the winter in Ireland.

ADULT

Water Rail

Rallus aquaticus
Rálóg uisce
FAIRLY COMMON RESIDENT. WINTER VISITOR (SEPTEMBER–MAY)
23–28 CM (BILL 3–4 CM)

The water rail, one of our most elusive birds, is seldom seen but often heard. Yet, there are an estimated 850 -1,700 breeding pairs in Ireland, twice as many as in Britain. Favoured habitats range from reed beds, swamps, fens and swampy borders to rivers, lakes and ponds with good vegetation cover, offered by rushes and reeds and other marsh plants. Pollardstown Fen, Co. Kildare, is one of the best places to encounter them. They are small, thin and lithe marsh birds, smaller than the moorhen, and dark brown above with slate-grey underparts. The red bill is disproportionately long. Its diagnostic call, known as "sharming" (derived from Norfolk) is emitted con gusto, especially during spring and summer, generally from dusk onwards. It is an anguished, piglet-like squeal, uttered many times. A sharp and metallic sounding "kek" is also repeated many times. Water rails are mainly resident in Ireland, but there is a substantial immigration of birds during autumn and winter, some from Iceland (four specimens of the Icelandic subspecies Rallus aquatics hibernans are in the National Museum) and others from the Continent (another four Museum specimens). It is the most frequently recorded non-passerine bird killed by striking lighthouses at night, especially at northern and north-western lighthouses during October and November, which led the famous Irish naturalist R.M.Barrington to postulate that they were Icelandic migrants. The northwards spring migration, as shown by mortalities at lighthouses, is focused along the east, rather than the west, coast.

ADULT

Coot

Fulica atra

Cearc cheannann

FAIRLY COMMON RESIDENT. WINTER VISITOR (OCTOBER–APRIL)
36–38 CM

The coot is a black, rotund and humpy-looking water bird with a white bill and a conspicuous white frontal shield. It is easily distinguished from the moorhen (p.129) by these characteristics and also by the lack of white undertail feathers. Juveniles are brownish-grey with a whitish throat and breast. The coot requires larger and more open water bodies than the moorhen, but also needs marginal vegetation for shelter and cover to build its bulky floating nest. The coot's common contact note is a very harsh, metallic and loud "tewk". They are very aggressive and quarrelsome birds, often engaging in vigorous skirmishes, in which the feet are used. They feed by diving and breaking off tender stalks of reed and other aquatic plants, especially Canadian pond weed. Less widespread and numerous than the moorhen, with approximately 8,600 birds during the breeding season, they occur most frequently in the north-east and on large Midland lakes. During the winter, their aggressiveness abates and they often gather in large flocks. In winter, there is a big influx of Continental birds, amounting to some 30,000 individuals, some of which may be responsible for extraordinarily large gatherings of up to 9,000 on Lough Corrib, Co. Galway in October and 2,000 on Lough Deravaragh, Co. Westmeath in November. Upwards of 8,000 winter on Loughs Neagh and Beg in Northern Ireland.

JUVENILE

ADULT

Snipe

Gallinago gallinago

Naoscach

COMMON RESIDENT, BREEDING NUMBERS DECLINING

COMMON WINTER VISITOR (OCTOBER–MARCH)

25–27 CM

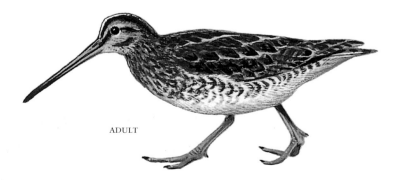

ADULT

The snipe is a secretive, shy bird, seldom seen on the ground. When flushed, it is identified in flight by its long, straight bill pointed slightly downwards, a richly patterned brown plumage, a towering zig-zag flight and a harsh rasping "scaap", repeated several times. Snipe, like woodcock (p.68), are crepuscular birds, spending the day resting or sleeping in marsh vegetation or coarse, damp pastures. Sometimes, several snipe will be flushed from a small area. After flying some distance, they will suddenly plunge down and land almost vertically in marshy vegetation. The size of our breeding population is unknown, but is in the order of 10,000 pairs, widely distributed in damp meadows, marshlands and pastures. From mid-March to mid-June, the birds quarter their breeding territory at dusk and during the night, calling their distinctive "chip-er, chip-er, chip-er" note, often interspersed with a unique drumming or bleating noise, produced by the rapid vibration of the outer tail feathers during a steep downward dive. Because of this noise, snipe are often known as "airy goats". During autumn and winter, there is a large immigration of snipe from the Baltic and other north European areas, as well as from Iceland.

See 'Waders' p.192

ADULT

Common Sandpiper

Actitis hypoleucos
Gobadán coiteann
LOCAL SUMMER VISITOR
APRIL–SEPTEMBER
19–21 CM

The common sandpiper has olive-brown upper parts, pure white underparts and is easily identified by its characteristic behaviour and call note. It is usually encountered flying low over lake water or along a stream or river in a stiff-winged, jerky flight consisting of alternate wing flickerings, followed by short glides on bowed wings. It has a conspicuous white wing bar extending almost across the full wing length. When in flight, it calls its shrill and loud "twee-wee-wee" and when standing on the ground, its rear end is constantly bobbing up and down, giving the impression of a hyperactive, short-tailed, plump wagtail. Common sandpipers, unlike other waders, are solitary birds, seldom encountered in flocks and widely spaced out during the breeding season. The estimated 2,500 pairs breeding in Ireland are mainly confined to west Kerry, Co. Cork, west Galway, Co. Mayo, Cos. Donegal and Fermanagh, with fewer birds in Cos. Antrim and Wicklow. While the common sandpiper sometimes occurs in lowland areas, it is essentially an upland species.

See 'Waders' p.192

ADULT

ADULT SUMMER

Black-headed Gull

Larus ridibundus

Sléibhín

COMMON RESIDENT

COMMON WINTER VISITOR (SEPTEMBER–APRIL)

34–37 CM

This gull is smaller than the common gull (opposite) and has a chocolate-brown head in summer only. In winter, the head is white with a dark patch behind the eye and a smaller smudge in the front. The slender bill and the legs are red, while the white edge of the wing extending to the tip is a good flight characteristic. There are 13,983 breeding pairs, including 10,107 in Northern Ireland, found in many large colonies on the margins of large inland lakes, in marshes on Midland bogs and along the coast. Outside the breeding season, these gulls disperse widely to feed on farmland, often following the plough to pick up insects, or in urban areas where they scavenge for food, while large numbers move to estuaries and harbours. They frequently roost on sports fields near the coast. Most Irish-bred birds remain in Ireland, with less than 10 per cent travelling abroad, mainly to Britain. Large numbers of northern European immigrants winter in Ireland and large winter concentrations have been recorded on the south coast (Cork Harbour and Clonakilty Bay), east coast (Dublin and Dundalk Bays), west coast (Shannon Estuary) and in Northern Ireland (Culmore Tip, Co. Derry, Belfast and Strangford Loughs).

See 'Terns & Smaller Gulls' p.169

ADULT WINTER

JUVENILE

ADULT SUMMER

Common Gull

Larus canus

Faoileán bán

LOCAL RESIDENT

COMMON WINTER VISITOR (SEPTEMBER–APRIL)

40–42 CM

The common gull could be confused with the herring gull (p.166), as both have pale grey upper parts, black wing tips with white spots and pale underparts. However, the common gull is distinguished by its smaller size and more delicate body, its quite different call, which is a sort of screaming "keeee-ya", and most importantly a greenish-yellow bill and legs. It is not very common in Ireland, with only 1,617 pairs, including 557 in Northern Ireland, mostly found breeding on islands in the large western lakes such as Loughs Corrib, Co. Galway; Carra, Mask, Conn and Carrowmore, Cos. Mayo and Gara, and Co. Sligo Land. They also breed in Cos. Donegal, Down and on many small marine islands off the west and north coasts. After breeding, most inland birds move to coastal areas, where considerably large flocks with many mottled brown juveniles (identified from other young gulls by a distinct black band on their white tail) gather, feeding mostly on earthworms in nearby pastures and roosting on the beach. A few Irish birds emigrate, but a much larger immigration takes place from Scotland, Scandinavia, Germany and Holland, Iceland and Russia. Apart from the west coast, coastal areas in counties Cork, Dublin, Louth and Down also have good numbers in winter.

See 'Terns & Smaller Gulls' p.169

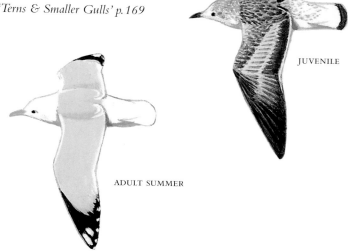

JUVENILE

ADULT SUMMER

Kingfisher

Alcedo atthis

Cruidín

Fairly common resident

16–17 CM

The kingfisher is an unmistakable, brilliantly coloured bird, often only seen as a flash of iridescent blue flying by before disappearing into the distance. Its flight is extremely fast, low and close to the water, whether along a stream, a river, a canal, a lake or an estuary. Perching on a branch or root overhanging water, it dives from it into the water for small fish. The kingfisher's upper parts are a dark greenish-blue, and the underparts are a warm chestnut. It has a white throat and neck patch, and its brilliant colouring may be an adaptation to warn off predators. Its call, a loud shrill "chee", repeated several times, often reveals the presence of the kingfisher before it is seen. Numbers in Ireland have decreased in recent years due to a number of different reasons. The estimated 1,300-2,100 breeding pairs are thinly scattered throughout the country on freshwater canals, sluggish rivers, streams and lakes. Most Irish kingfishers are sedentary, moving less than 10 km from their breeding areas. However, some birds move to nearby coastal estuaries in the autumn and winter, where they spend the winter months.

ADULT MALE

ADULT FEMALE

Sand Martin

Riparia riparia
Gabhlán gainimh
SUMMER VISITOR (MARCH–OCTOBER)
12 CM

The sand martin is smaller than the house martin (p.35) and swallow (p.34) and is easily identified by its uniform, dark earth-brown upper parts and white underparts with a brown band across the breast. The tail is shorter than the swallow's and only slightly forked. The flight of the sand martin is more fluttering and less sophisticated than the graceful swoopings of the swallow. Martins frequently give a short "tchirrp" call in flight. They are very gregarious and are often seen feeding in small groups over water, where flies and beetles are caught. Widespread throughout the country, they nest in small colonies of usually less than 100 pairs in gravel or sandpits. Horizontal tunnels, up to 1m deep, are excavated in the face of the sand bank and a nest is made in a chamber at the tunnel end. There have been recent population crashes (1968–9 and 1983–4), associated with severe droughts in the African Sahel, close to the wintering grounds. Despite these declines, some 50,000–150,000 pairs breed in Ireland. The autumn passage back to Africa starts in July, and small parties move south along the Irish coast until mid-September.

ADULT

ADULT

Grey Wagtail

Motacilla cinerea
Glasóg liath
FAIRLY COMMON RESIDENT. PASSAGE MIGRANT (AUGUST–OCTOBER)
18–19 CM

Despite its name, the grey wagtail is very yellow, with a brilliant yellow breast in summer and yellow under-tail feathers contrasting with blue-grey upper parts. The male has a black throat, whitish stripes above and below the eye and a long black tail. During the breeding season, the wagtails' favoured habitat are fast-flowing and rocky streams in upland areas, but they also occur on more sluggish lowland rivers, where there are weirs and locks to speed up water movement. They fly and flit about, frequently calling their contact note "tzi–tzi", and perch on boulders along the water courses. They are active and busy birds with a bobbing tail. About 22,000 breeding pairs are scattered throughout Ireland and occur in every county, with greater abundance in upland areas. They nest in holes or cavities in walls or rocky ledges, especially under bridges. After breeding, the birds move to lowland areas in a southerly direction. There is evidence of an autumn passage along the south coast, but it is not known whether these are Irish or immigrant birds. Birds on passage are even more vocal than usual. One Scottish ringed bird has been recovered in Ireland.

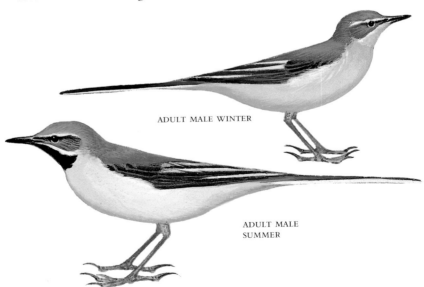

ADULT MALE WINTER

ADULT MALE
SUMMER

Dipper

Cinclus cinclus hibernicus
Gabha dubh
FAIRLY COMMON RESIDENT
18 CM

JUVENILE

The dipper is a plump, short-tailed bird found typically along swift streams or mountain rivers. Its upper parts are dark brown and its conspicuous white throat, as well as its aquatic habits, distinguish it from other birds. It frequently "bobs" when perched on a rock in, or near, water, and it is the only perching bird (i.e. with feet adapted for perching as with half the birds of the world) that is aquatic. It plunges into the water and walks or swims against the current while feeding on insects, gathered by upturning stones on the bottom. The special Irish subspecies (which also occurs on the Isle of Man and in western Scotland) has a darker, chocolate-brown crown and nape and the rest of its upper parts are much darker. The rufous of the breast is also duller, darker and more restricted. The ordinary call of the dipper is a loud "zit–zit–zit", the song is a liquid warbling interspersed with some harsh notes. An estimated 1,750–5,000 pairs breed in Ireland, mainly along streams and rivers, especially in upland areas. However, many breed also in lowlands, particularly in the western areas. The dipper is generally absent from the sluggish Midland rivers.

ADULT

Sedge Warbler

Acrocephalus schoenobaenus

Ceoiaire cibe

COMMON SUMMER VISITOR (APRIL–SEPTEMBER)

13 CM

This small brown warbler has a creamy white eye-stripe and black-brown streaks on the crown and back. Its rump is tawny and unstreaked. Its underparts are creamy white. The sedge warbler first announces its presence in April, by a loud vigorous torrent of song, delivered while perched on a bush top or during its song flight, when the bird flies up almost vertically in the air, turns suddenly to descend with spread wings and tail and returns to its perch. The sedge warbler's song is a rapid sequence of repeated chatterings, musical notes, trills and mimicry. As it sometimes sings at night, it is often mistaken for a nightingale. It has a skulking, furtive behaviour, creeping around in dense undergrowth. Totalling about 110,000 breeding pairs throughout Ireland, it is found in lowland marsh and wet habitats and now frequently in young forestry plantations, but also in coastal areas, especially along river valleys. There has been a corresponding loss of birds in recent years, from approximately the same areas where the reed bunting (opposite) has declined.

See 'Warblers' p.71

ADULT

Reed Bunting

Emberiza schoeniclus
Gealóg ghiolcaí
COMMON RESIDENT
15–16 CM

The male is immediately identified by its bold, black head and throat, its white collar and dark brown upper parts. The female is drabber, with a brown head and black and white moustachial streaks. Both sexes have streaky brown upper parts and white outer tail feathers, which are conspicuous in flight. Reed buntings are usually seen flitting about and perching in reed beds, hedges, scrub and other low bushes near water or wet areas. In recent years, reed buntings have been moving into drier habitats created by young forestry plantations, and they sometimes visit garden bird tables in winter. During the breeding season, their song is a squeaky "tweek-tweek-tweek-tititick", sung from a perch. Although the reed bunting is common and widespread, with an estimated 130,000 pairs, most abundantly found in low lying areas, it has lately become curiously scarce or absent from a swath of countryside, extending south-west of north Wexford to Cork and south Kerry. After breeding, there are some local dispersals with few, if any, birds leaving Ireland. Some north European birds may visit this country during winter, as there is evidence of some passage in October and March from coastal bird observatories.

See 'Sparrows & Buntimgs' p.21

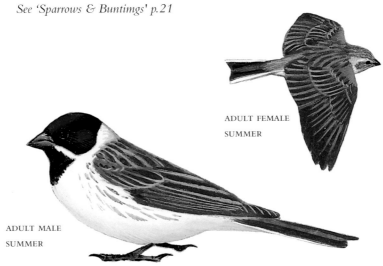

ADULT FEMALE
SUMMER

ADULT MALE
SUMMER

Coastal Areas

*Banna Strand,
Co. Kerry, where
oystercatchers,
sanderlings, turnstone
and ringed plover are
often seen.*

The Irish coastline is extremely diverse, with a complete range of habitats – extending from towering, Atlantic-facing cliffs to sandy, sheltered beaches, rocky to soft shorelines, estuaries, bays, lagoons, loughs, a fjord (Killary Harbour in Co. Mayo), drowned river valleys, shallow and deep inshore waters, to numerous offshore islands.

Some of the most exciting places to visit in summer are seabird colonies, generally located on offshore islands or on rugged coastal cliffs. There the birds are easily observed through their entire breeding cycle, along with their associated behaviour and interaction with other seabirds.

At places such as the Saltee Islands, Co. Wexford, or the Cliffs of Moher, Co. Clare, myriads of kittiwakes, puffins, fulmars, razorbills, guillemots, the three large gulls and many more birds can be seen flying to and from their breeding ledges or nesting sites – courting and fighting, building their nests, incubating eggs and feeding their chicks. Our largest breeding seabird, the gannet, is frequently seen searching inshore

Great Saltee Island, Co. Wexford. Ireland's most famous island for easy observation of breeding sea birds.

waters for mackerel, herring and cod. Two of the other frequently encountered birds inshore are the Manx shearwaters, slicing the waves with their stiff wings, and the storm petrels, performing their ballet-like flight in search of plankton and fish offal. Mixed breeding colonies of the Arctic and common terns occur on offshore islands in Connemara, while little terns nest on pebbly beaches, particularly along the east coast. Shags and cormorants, which seek breeding refuge from human disturbance on offshore islands, are likely to be seen inshore when patrolling the waters in search of sand eels and plump wrass.

Amongst the soft shorelines, estuaries are some of the most rewarding places to visit. During the winter, large numbers of waders such as dunlin, ringed plover, knot, sanderling, oystercatchers, bar-tailed godwit, redshank and greenshank can be seen feeding on mudflats rich in invertebrate food, each of them employing a different feeding technique, related to the shape and length of their bills, and exploiting different parts of the estuary with the common objective of making the most of the food resources. Among the larger birds, the pale-breasted brent goose plucks sea lettuce off mudflats or eel grass from the muddy bottom in shallow waters by dipping its head or "upending" like ducks. Sometimes wigeon behave in an opportunistic manner and remain in the vicinity of the geese, picking up scraps of uneaten eel grass.

Rocky shores appeal to other wading birds. Along the rocky sections of the west and north coast, turnstones are frequently found along with purple sandpipers and oystercatchers. In the inshore waters, great northern and red-throated divers lurk low like battleships, occasionally plunging down for small fish below, while packs of common scoter, sometimes near red-breasted mergansers, congregate and bob on the surface like corks at the mouth of shallow estuaries. Further out, eiders, long-tailed ducks and black guillemots – all in their confusing black-and-white winter plumages – brave choppier seas.

Red-throated Diver

Gavia stellata

Lóma rua

VERY RARE LOCAL BREEDER PASSAGE MIGRANT AND WINTER VISITOR
(SEPTEMBER–MAY)

53–69 CM

The red-throated diver is widely distributed in Irish coastal waters during winter. The best-distinguishing feature between the red-throated and the closely related great northern diver (p.146) is the slender, upturned bill, which is apparent at a distance. Also, the red throat has a paler grey plumage, finely speckled with white. Red-throated divers occur in ones and twos, particularly in shallow, sandy-bottomed areas where they dive for flat fish. Up to 1,000 birds winter in Ireland, with concentrations in the shallow sandy bays in Counties Wexford, Dublin, Louth and south Down. The Shannon Estuary, Galway Bay, and the Broadhaven and Killala bays, Co. Mayo, also carry good numbers. The bulk of the wintering birds come from the Scottish breeding population, many of which move into Ireland between late August and mid-September. Some continue south to France. Other winter visitors possibly come from Iceland, Greenland and Scandinavia. But the red-throated diver also occurs in this country as a rare breeding species, with an estimated 6–8 pairs in 1997, but only 3–4 pairs in 2002 in the moorland loughs of Co. Donegal. Birds in breeding plumage have a grey head and a smart, red throat patch. Their grey upper parts are not speckled during the summer.

See 'Divers' p.146

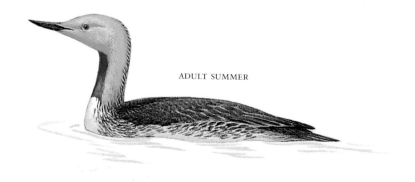

ADULT SUMMER

Great Northern Diver

Gavia immer

Lóma mór

Winter visitor (September–May)

69–91 CM

ADULT WINTER

The great northern diver is more numerous and widespread in Irish coastal waters than the red-throated diver (p.145). In winter its upper parts are dark grey-brown without any white speckling, contrasting with a white throat. It differs from the red-throated diver by its larger size, thicker neck, a larger angular head and a noticeably bigger and heavier bill. In March, some adults show signs of breeding plumage, with a black head, an incomplete white neck collar and large white spots on dark upper parts. Their prolonged and mournful wailing can sometimes be heard in the autumn and spring. Less confined to shallow inland waters than the red-throated diver, the great northern is equally happy in deeper water and is sometimes found as far as 10 km from the coast. Numbers are highest off the west coast from Cos. Donegal to Cork, with fewer along the east coast. At least 1,500 birds come to Ireland in winter but, in the absence of ringing recoveries, their origin is uncertain. Numbers wintering in Ireland are larger than the breeding population in Iceland (100–300 pairs), so Greenland and Canadian birds are probably involved.

See 'Divers' below

DIVERS

- dive by sliding under head first, submerge when alarmed
- fly fast, with head and neck lower than rest of the body
- nest on the ground, beside open-shored loughs
- winter on the sea
- can be distinguished by bill shape and head posture

Fulmar

Fulmarus glacialis
Fulmaire
COMMON RESIDENT
45–50 CM

ADULT

The fulmar looks superficially like a gull, but has a quite different flight behaviour. Fulmars glide effortlessly along cliffs and over water on stiffly extended wings, banking and turning to take every advantage of the wind currents. When gliding they will sometimes flap their wings but they can also "hang" by using their webbed feet as rudders and flexing their wings to hold position. The fulmar's underparts are white and the upper parts are grey; it lacks the black wing tips of the gull. Its neck is short and stubby. Close up, a nasal tube on top of the bill can be seen. Fulmars are widespread around the coast – there are 38,625 breeding pairs, of which 5,992 occur in Northern Ireland. They are all in coastal counties, nesting on cliffs, headlands and islands. Because their legs are set so far back on their body, they are unable to launch themselves into flight from the flat ground and must, therefore, nest on, or close to, cliff faces. Fulmars first bred in Ireland in 1911, and their expansion and colonization of the coastline has been remarkable. They are long-lived, with a life expectancy of about 35 years, and generally do not breed until they are about eight years old.

See 'Gull-type Birds' p. 163

ADULT

Sooty Shearwater

Puffinus griseus.

Cánóg dhorcha

PASSAGE MIGRANT (MAINLY AUGUST–OCTOBER)

40–51 CM

ADULT

Distinguished from all other shearwaters by a uniform, sooty-brown plumage and an indistinct, pale white strip along the centre of the under-wing. At a distance it looks all black. Its body is heavier than the Manx shearwater, with longer, thinner wings. Breeding in the southern hemisphere, it migrates northwards in autumn to feed in the northern Atlantic waters, occurring in Irish inland coastal waters, mainly off the west coast. Normally seen in small numbers of 1–20, but during favourable weather big numbers, upwards of several thousands, can be observed. The best location to see them is off Cape Clear Island, Co. Cork, between late August and early September. Other good observation spots are headlands and islands along the north-western, western and south-western coasts: Bloody Foreland and Malin Head, Co. Donegal; Kilcummin Head and Annagh Head, Co. Mayo; Bridges of Ross, Loop Head and Mizen Head, Co. Clare; Brandon Point, Co. Kerry; and The Old Head of Kinsale, Co. Cork.

Great Shearwater

Puffinus gravis

Cánóg mhór

UNCOMMON PASSAGE MIGRANT (JULY–OCTOBER)

43–51 CM

ADULT

This southern hemisphere breeder may be seen at the same inshore locations as the sooty shearwater. It has a dark cap, contrasting with the white throat and collar, and a body that is overall dark brown above and white below, with a narrow white patch at the base of the tail, features that separate it from other shearwaters.

Manx Shearwater

Puffinus puffinus

Cánóg dhubh

COMMON LOCAL BREEDER PASSAGE MIGRANT (MAINLY MARCH–OCTOBER)

30–38 CM

Like the storm petrel (p.150), Manx shearwaters are most likely to be seen at sea. They are black above and white below, creating a sharp contrast when the birds are gliding low over the water and banking over waves. Their flight is sometimes leisurely, sometimes fast, with much gliding on stiff wings and occasional wingbeats. When the sea is rough they follow the wave contours, exposing their contrasting plumage as they twist, turn and bank along the waves. The Manx shearwater comes ashore to its breeding colonies in March–August. There are 37,178 breeding pairs, of which 4,633 occur in Northern Ireland. They breed on a few marine islands off the Kerry, Galway, Antrim, Down, Dublin and Wexford coasts. A few breed on Wicklow Head. Most of the population breeds in Co. Kerry, with large numbers on Puffin Island (6,400 pairs), Skellig Michael, Inishnabro (5,600 pairs), Inishtearaght, Inishvickillane and Inishtooskert. The birds are strictly nocturnal on the breeding sites, spending the day either in their burrows or at sea. As with the fulmar (p.147), their legs are located far back on the body, making it difficult to take off unless there is a wind or high point to launch themselves from. After the breeding season, the birds wander widely in the Atlantic. Irish birds have been recovered in various places, including Brazil, Uruguay, Argentina, Michigan (USA), Canada and Switzerland.

ADULT

ADULT

Storm Petrel

Hydrobates pelagicus
Guairdeall
COMMON LOCAL BREEDER.
PASSAGE MIGRANT (APRIL–OCTOBER)
14–18 CM

The smallest of our seabirds, with a distinct sooty-black plumage and a conspicuous white rump, the storm petrel is nearly always seen from a boat out at sea, flitting and dancing almost bat-like over the water, occasionally dipping down to pick up small animal remains in the plankton or tiny pieces of offal. Sometimes it seems to walk on the water, like the biblical St. Peter, from whom the name "petrel" may have been derived. Like other petrels, storm petrels are essentially pelagic, living for months in the open Atlantic, sheltering in the troughs between the waves during storms. Only coming to shore – from May to October – to breed on remote islands, they often nest in large numbers in loose stones, old stone walls, abandoned stone buildings and sometimes in soil burrows. They come ashore at night. There are some 99,950 breeding pairs specifically located on west-coast islands, from Cos. Kerry to Donegal, including 26,000 pairs on Inishtooskert, Co. Kerry, the largest colony in the world. Most breeding birds leave the coastal waters by the beginning of October and move further out into the Atlantic. Recoveries of Irish birds point to west and southern Africa as main wintering areas.

ADULT

ADULT

ADULT

Gannet

Morus bassanus
Gainéad
COMMON LOCAL BREEDER
87–100 CM

2ND/3RD YEAR ADULT

ADULT WINTER

4TH WINTER ADULT

The adult gannet is the largest white-and-black seabird in our coastal waters. It is easily identified by the extensive black tips at the end of its long wings, which span 2 m. The gannet's neck is long and its pointed bill is generally directed downwards as the bird surveys the sea for herring, mackerel and other fish. It plunge-dives spectacularly into the sea with its wings folded back, often from a height of some 30 m. Fish are speared by the gannet on its return to the surface. Immature birds are dusky brown, speckled with white. This plumage, very different from that of the adult, can be confusing. Young gannets become progressively white, until attaining full plumage in their fourth year. Gannets are scarcest in coastal waters from December to February, when the bulk of the population has moved south to the north and west African waters. There are five breeding colonies, which held 32,758 breeding pairs in 1999 – the last two having been established in 1978 and 1989, respectively. The most recently available figures for each colony are: Little Skellig, Co. Kerry (26,850 pairs); Bull Rock, Co. Cork (1,815 pairs); Great Saltee, Co. Wexford (1,250 pairs); Clare Island, Co. Mayo (2–3 pairs); and Ireland's Eye, Co. Dublin (188 pairs). Irish juvenile gannets travel further south than the adults during the winter, moving to the Mediterranean and west Africa.

ADULT SUMMER

Cormorant

Phalacrocorax carbo

Broigheall

COMMON RESIDENT, INCREASING

80–100 CM

JUVENILE

The cormorant is distinguished
from the similar-looking shag
(opposite) by its white chin and cheeks.
During the breeding season, it also has a
conspicuous, white thigh patch, which is noticeable
in flight. At close range, its plumage is bronze-brown and
black. Essentially maritime, many cormorants occur on inland lakes and
rivers – especially during the autumn and winter – to which they are
attracted by the more abundant fish population. There are also several inland
breeding colonies where birds nest, somewhat bizarrely, in trees. In the
water, cormorants hold their heads tilted upwards, in contrast to the shag's
more horizontally held position. There are 5,211 breeding pairs, including
663 in Northern Ireland; they are widely scattered across many colonies
situated on islands around the coast and at nine inland sites. Numbers have
increased recently as the bird is now a protected species. Food eaten by the
cormorant is greatly determined by what is available; under certain
conditions, cormorants can also damage fisheries. Some migration occurs
in the autumn, when about a quarter of all young birds ringed on Little
Saltee, Co. Wexford, travel to France, Spain and Portugal.

ADULT SUMMER

Shag

Phalacrocorax aristotelis

Seaga

COMMON RESIDENT

65–80 CM

JUVENILE

The shag and the cormorant (opposite) can be easily confused. Both are large black birds frequently seen in coastal waters, often standing on rocks with outspread wings. The shag, however, is smaller and has a thinner bill; it does not have any white on its face and also lacks the white thigh patch of the cormorant. Closer up, the shag has a green-black plumage and during the breeding season, a small, upstanding head crest can be seen. Shags are essentially marine and only rarely occur on freshwater lakes or rivers. Young birds are brown and, unlike the juvenile cormorants, do not have any white on their chest. There are 3,727 breeding pairs, including 301 in Northern Ireland, breeding on rocky islands off the coast, along sea cliffs, or under boulders. Breeding birds vigorously defend their nests, sitting tight and lunging at intruders with an open yellow mouth, hissing and grunting. Birds disperse along the coast after the breeding season; very few travel overseas and those that do, go mainly to Scotland and Wales. Shags feed by diving to near the sea bottom, usually catching sand eels. Severe winter storms sometimes drive shags inland, causing high mortality at sea.

ADULT

Barnacle Goose

Branta leucopsis

Gé ghiúrainn

LOCAL FERAL RESIDENT, RARE

LOCAL WINTER VISITOR (OCTOBER–APRIL)

58–70 CM

ADULT

Barnacle geese can be identified at a distance by their sharply contrasting black-and-white plumage – evoking images of prim Victorian spinsters dressed in black velvet-and-white lace, their closely packed grazing flocks feeding on grass swards, and also by their characteristic barking calls that sound like a pack of whelping terriers. They are smaller than the great black-backed gulls (p.167), which are often nearby, and their conspicuous white face and forehead contrast with a glossy black crown, neck and breast. The upper parts are greyish, barred with black and fringed with white in adults. The first winter birds have, until the following April, distinct pale-brown borders to the wing coverts. The bill is small and dainty, and the legs are black. Barnacles are very gregarious. The Irish wintering flocks belong to the Greenland breeding stock, which retains wintering grounds in Europe separate from those of the lot breeding in Svalbard, the Baltic and arctic Russia. A total of 56,386 Greenland barnacle geese were counted in Ireland and Scotland in April 2003. There were 9,043 in Ireland, scattered in flocks on remote west and north-coast islands. There are also a few coastal mainland haunts, with about 1,500 at Lissadell-Ballintemple, Co. Sligo.

See 'Geese' p.120

ADULT

Common Scoter

Melanitta nigra

Scótar

LOCAL BREEDER, RARE, DECLINING. WINTER VISITOR (OCTOBER–APRIL)

44–54 CM

The common scoter is an unspectacular-looking sea duck that occurs in coastal waters during the winter, but is also a rare breeder in a few freshwater lakes. During the winter, they are often seen as small black ducks bobbing up and down in straggly flocks offshore, especially in areas of sandy seabeds and shallows where they dive to pick up mussels, other bivalve molluscs and sand eels. The drake is entirely black, but close up, the bill has a conspicuous yellow patch. The female is browner with pale buff cheeks. Up to 12,000 birds winter in Irish waters and probably come from Iceland, north Russia, Sweden and Finland. Largest concentrations are found off the east and west coasts, with the biggest flocks at Wexford Bay, Co. Wexford; Donegal Bay, Co. Donegal; Castlemaine Harbour and Rossbehy, Co. Kerry and the Nanny Estuary, Co. Meath. A small breeding population (80 pairs in 1999) is concentrated in four lowland lakes: Lough Corrib, Co. Galway; Lough Conn and Lough Cullin, Co. Mayo; and Lough Ree, Co. Roscommon.

See 'Ducks' p. 120–1

ADULT
FEMALE

ADULT MALE

Eider

Somateria mollissima

Éadar

LOCAL RESIDENT, INCREASING.

WINTER VISITOR (SEPTEMBER–APRIL)

50–71 CM

ADULT
FEMALE

If a large black-and-white duck paired to a warm brown one are seen off the north coast, they will almost certainly be eider ducks. Eiders are long, heavy-bodied sea ducks with a flattish head and large bill. The male has a boldly contrasting black belly and a white back. Its crown is black. The female is uniformly rufous brown, with closely spaced black barring, creating an almost mottled appearance. Since they first colonised the remote island of Inishstrahull, off the north coast of Donegal, in 1912, eiders have been gradually spreading south, down the west and east coasts, and there are now about 600–1,000 pairs breeding in those areas. They are frequently seen off the Donegal coast, especially in the vicinity of small offshore islands, which are used as breeding grounds. They are also regularly observed off the Antrim and north Down coasts, where they breed as well. There is a flourishing colony on Inishmurray, Co. Sligo. County Mayo has recently (2001) been colonised. The eiders also bred in Co. Kerry in 1981, and possibly subsequently too. Single birds or small parties winter off the south coast.

See 'Ducks' p. 120–1

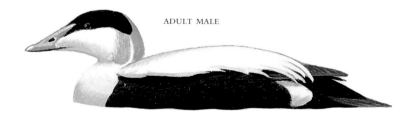

ADULT MALE

Long-tailed Duck

Clangula hyemalis

Lacha earrfhada

LOCALLY UNCOMMON WINTER VISITOR (OCTOBER–APRIL)

40–47 CM

ADULT
FEMALE
WINTER

The long-tailed duck is a winter visitor to coastal waters, especially to the north-western areas, and usually occurs in parties of less than ten. The male is a startling combination of white and dark brown, with a long, pointed tail. It was once called the "sea pheasant" by wildfowlers. The male's head, neck and flanks are white, with a dark-brown patch on the side of the neck. The head and the bill are small. In flight, the dark-brown upper parts of the wings contrast with the white sides of the back. The female is generally brown, with white cheeks and a smaller, dark cheek spot. The only other piebald bird that might be seen in the vicinity of the long-tailed duck is the black guillemot (p.177) in winter plumage. Long-tailed duck numbers have been increasing in recent years, with about 2,000 wintering in our coastal waters. The largest numbers are found off the coasts of Cos. Donegal, Sligo, Mayo, Galway, Clare, Wexford and Dublin, and in Carlingford Lough, Co. Louth and Belfast Lough, Co. Down. Highest numbers occur from December until mid-February. Irish wintering birds probably come from Russian and Fennoscandinavian breeding populations.

See 'Ducks' p.120–1

ADULT MALE WINTER

Red-breasted Merganser

Mergus serrator

Síolta rua

UNCOMMON LOCAL BREEDER. WINTER VISITOR (SEPTEMBER–MAY)

52–58 CM

When sitting on water, the red-breasted merganser has a low and long profile, with a very thin bill. Males have a dark-green head with a crest at the back. A wide white collar separates the head from the chestnut breast. The flanks are grey. The duck merganser has a reddish head with a crest, and brownish-grey upper parts, without a white collar. Both birds have an extensive, central, white wing patch stretching from the front to the back of the wing. This feature is very prominent in flight. Red-breasted mergansers essentially occur in estuaries, or at the entrances thereof; they are also sometimes found offshore in shallow, sandy-bottomed waters. About 2,000–3,000 of them winter in Ireland. They are well distributed around the coastline, except off cliff areas. Large wintering numbers are recorded in Inner Galway Bay; Wexford Harbour and Slobs; Cork Harbour; Lough Swilly, Co. Donegal; Strangford Lough, Co. Down and Larne Lough, Co. Antrim. About 700 pairs breed in sheltered lakes and large rivers, mainly in the north-western and western areas, and particularly in Cos. Mayo and Galway. Very few are found south of a line between Limerick and Dundalk.

See 'Ducks' p. 120–1

ADULT FEMALE

ADULT MALE

Purple Sandpiper

Calidris maritima

Gobadán cosbhuí

<small>LOCAL WINTER VISITOR (AUGUST–APRIL)</small>

20–22 CM

The purple sandpiper is a robust and rotund, small, undistinguished-looking, dark-plumaged wader with dull yellow legs. An extraordinarily tame bird, it stands immobile on rocks and can be easily overlooked. The head, upper parts and chest are slate-grey, sometimes showing a faint purple gloss. When seen close up, the base of the bill is yellow. The belly is white, with dark markings on the flanks. When disturbed off their rocks, purple sandpipers call a high-pitched and nervous "tritt-tritt-tritt". The first purple sandpipers start arriving on Irish coasts in August, from their arctic breeding grounds in Iceland, Greenland and probably Canada. Their numbers build up to a total of about 2,000 birds. They are most frequently seen on the Mayo coastline and islands, while smaller numbers occur in Co. Galway, and good numbers in Co. Clare and north Kerry. North Co. Donegal and the coastlines of Cos. Antrim and Down hold many, while fewer are recorded further south on the less rocky east coast. The south coast has only very few. While flocks of over 100 have been recorded, smaller groups of up to 20 individuals are more common.

See 'Waders' p.192

WINTER

WINTER

Turnstone

Arenaria interpres

Piardalai tra

COMMON WINTER VISITOR (JULY–MAY)

22–24 CM

WINTER

In winter the turnstone has mottled brown upper parts and white underparts, with a dark and broad breast band. Its bill is short and its legs, orange. The pied flight pattern helps to distinguish it from the purple sandpiper (p.159), which is also found on rocky shorelines, often in mixed flocks with turnstones. Some birds returning from their arctic breeding grounds in the early autumn still retain the contrasting black-and-white head pattern and orange-brown upper parts, making them look much brighter and smarter than they do in their winter plumage. Turnstones are tough, muscular-looking waders, very busy and active on the shore, flicking over small pebbles to expose the insects underneath. They also root amongst decaying seaweed for sandhoppers. They are often very noisy, calling a quick "tuck-a-tuk" and a long rapid trill. About 10,000 birds winter in Ireland, widely scattered around the coastline, with the largest numbers on the west coast – from Cos. Sligo to Kerry, and on the east coast – from Cos. Antrim to Dublin. Small groups of up to 20 birds are not unusual, with some flocks even exceeding 100 birds. Our birds come from the Greenland and Canadian breeding grounds. A few birds remain in Ireland during the summer.

See 'Waders' p.192

WINTER

Great Skua

Catharacta skua

Meirleach mór

Recent rare breeder. Passage migrant (August–October, smaller numbers March–May)

53–58 cm

ADULT

About the size of a Herring Gull, but with a heavier body and shorter wings. Plumage is dark brown, with white wing patches that "flash" during flight. Fast and agile flier, frequently chasing other seabirds in piratical manner, forcing them to regurgitate food, which is then eaten by the skua. Since sea-watching commenced in the 1960s, these skuas have been shown to be regular passage birds, especially off the west coast, travelling to and from their nesting grounds in Iceland, Faeroes and north Scotland. Three Icelandic and three Scottish ringed birds have been recovered in Ireland. Largest numbers have been observed off Cape Clear Island, Co. Cork, peak movements being in the first half of April and September – 1,000+ individuals have been recorded in one day. Numbers observed along the east coast are much smaller. A suspected breeding pair occurred on two west coast islands in 2000. The first birds bred (one downy chick) in 2001. More pairs will probably follow, provided they are undisturbed.

Arctic Skua

Stercorarius parasiticus

Meirleach Artach

Passage migrant (occurring mainly between April and October)

41–46 cm

The most frequently seen skua, principally off the west coast, sometimes wandering inland. Often in small migratory packs, but more usually as singles. Smaller than the great skua, its wings are longer and narrower; its dashing

DARK PHASE

PALE PHASE

flight, when chasing terns or gulls, is falconesque. It has two long, pointed tail feathers. Wide plumage variation, from dark to pale.

Little Gull

Larus minutus

Sléibhín beag

Passage migrant and winter visitor. Occurs in all months.

25–27 cm

ADULT
SUMMER

The smallest gull, resembling a miniature black-headed gull. In summer the head is jet black, the bill and legs, red. Underwings are dark, bordered by white on trailing edges, contrasting with grey upper wings. In winter, adults and immatures lack the black head but retain some head smudging, and have a black spot behind the eye. Immatures have a black "zigzag" pattern on the upper wings; the underwings are pale. The tail is slightly forked, with a black subterminal bar. Their flight is agile and tern-like, and wings slightly rounded. They feed on small fish, crustaceans, etc., taken from the water surface. They also catch insects on the wing. Once considered a great rarity (only 15 records to 1950), they are now regular winter visitors, especially to the Wicklow and Wexford coastlines. Large autumn and winter influxes recorded on the east coast (500+ were seen at Wicklow Harbour in November 2000). Formerly reported only from Galway Bay on the west coast, now regular in some other western counties, especially Kerry and Clare. Our birds probably originate from the expanding Baltic and Russian breeding populations.

See 'Terns & smallers gulls' p.169

Mediterranean Gull

Larus melanocephalus

Sléibhín Meánmhuirí

Summer visitor and rare breeder, increasing

36–38 cm

ADULT
SUMMER

Formerly a scarce visitor, now a rare breeder (since 1996) with up to three pairs in Co. Wexford and two pairs in Northern Ireland. The Mediterranean gull is about the size of, and similarly plumaged, as the black-headed gull (though a little stouter). Distinguished by the absence of black tips to the white primary wing feathers, during all seasons.

See 'Terns & smallers gulls' p.169

GULL-TYPE BIRDS OF ROCKY COASTLINE

In decreasing order of size:
The five large gulls – glaucous (p.165), Iceland (p.165), great black–backed (p.167), herring (p.166) and lesser black–backed (p.164)
- stand tall and walk readily
- fly with strong wingbeats, usually showing a bend at front of wing
- adults have yellow bills with a red spot
- adults have very dark wing tips with white spots, except glaucous and Iceland gulls
- adults are distinguished by colour of back and legs
- young birds are mottled grey-brown and difficult to distinguish

Fulmars (p.147)
- characteristically squat with legs hidden
- glide with straight wings
- have a "tube" on upper surface of bill, with no red spot
- uniformly coloured on back, wings and tail
- have no black on wing tips

Kittiwakes (p.168)
- have short black legs
- have yellow-green bills, red inside the mouth
- have black wing tips without white spots

Arctic terns (p.173)
- have slim bodies, narrow wings and deeply forked tails
- have short red legs, black caps and blood-red bills
- have no black on wing tips

JUVENILE HERRING GULL

Lesser Black-backed Gull

Larus fuscus

Droimneach beag

SUMMER VISITOR (FEBRUARY–SEPTEMBER)

WINTER VISITOR, INCREASING (AUGUST–FEBRUARY)

52–67 CM

The lesser black-backed gull, unlike its four close relatives – the great black-backed gull (p.167), herring gull (p.166), glaucous gull (opposite) and Iceland gull (opposite), is generally a summer visitor, although an increasing number winter in Ireland. Yellow legs and slate-grey upper parts distinguish this gull from the others. Sometimes, however, the legs of subadults in winter are flesh-coloured. They occur in the same coastal areas as the herring gulls, but they also breed inland on islands in large freshwater lakes – Lough Neagh, Co. Antrim; Lough Erne, Co. Fermanagh; Lough Corrib, Co. Galway; Lough Derg, Co. Donegal; Lough Gara, Co. Sligo and Lough Mask, Co. Mayo. There are 4,849 breeding pairs, of which 1,973 are in Northern Ireland. They are almost equally divided between inland and coastal locations, in colonies that can be quite large. Lesser black-backs start to arrive back from their wintering grounds in Iberia and north Africa in mid-February, and depart again in August–October. The several thousand wintering in Ireland are concentrated in the Wicklow, Wexford and Cork coastal areas, as well as at many inland sites, particularly in the east, south and north-eastern parts of the country.

See 'Gull-type Birds' p.163

ADULT

Glaucous Gull

Larus hyperboreus

Faoileán glas

UNCOMMON WINTER VISITOR (NOVEMBER–FEBRUARY) BUT RECORDED IN ALL MONTHS.

62–68 CM

ADULT SUMMER

Our largest visiting gull, appearing in increasing numbers during recent years and generally easy to distinguish from other gulls. Upwards of 200 birds, mostly singles, occur each year. Adults have pale grey back and upper wings, with the rest of the body a striking white. The head is big and heavy; the yellow bill is stout, tipped by a black spot. The legs are flesh pink. Immature birds have a more uniform plumage; first-year birds are a pale creamy brown, less dark than most other immature gulls and with wing tips paler than rest of the wing. As they age their plumage becomes progressively whiter. Our birds probably originate from the populations in the arctic regions in east Greenland, Iceland (one ringed as a pullus in June 1982 was found dead at Ballycotton, Co. Cork, March 1983) and northwestern Russia. Fishing ports (Killybegs, Co. Donegal: Galway Harbour, and Rossaveal, Co. Galway: Dingle, Co. Kerry), landfill sites (Newport and Ballina, Co. Mayo; Rogerstown Estuary, Co. Dublin; Culmore. Co. Derry), and other favoured locations (Poulnasherry Bay, Co.Clare), especially along the west coast, are good places to see these gulls.

See 'Gull-type Birds' p.163

Iceland Gull

Larus glaucoides

Faoileán Íoslannach

UNCOMMON WINTER VISITOR (NOVEMBER–FEBRUARY)

52–60 CM

ADULT SUMMER

Breeds in west and east Greenland, north-east Canada and north-west Russia. Their plumage is similar to the glaucous gull, but they are markedly smaller in size, with a less heavy bill. Upwards of 300 occur each winter, generally at the same locations as the glaucous gull.

See 'Gull-type Birds' p.163

Herring Gull

Larus argentatus

Faoileán scadán

COMMON RESIDENT, RECENT DECREASE

WINTER VISITOR (AUGUST–MAY)

55–67 CM

ADULT SUMMER

The herring gull is the commonest sea gull of the coastline and a frequent inland visitor, especially to refuse dumps and freshly ploughed land. It has pale grey upper parts and black-and-white wing tips. The legs are flesh-pink, unlike those of the common gull (p.135). "Kyow" is the ordinary call and when the birds are disturbed during the nesting season, they make a deep "gah-gah-gah". Herring gulls are more adaptable than other gulls, nesting on buildings in urban areas and feeding on a wide range of foods. Numbers in Ireland have declined drastically from about 60,000 pairs in 1969 to about 44,000 pairs in 1987, and only 6,235 breeding pairs, including 714 in Northern Ireland, today. It is thought that botulism poisoning, picked up from eating putrefying meat in rubbish dumps, has been a major factor in this mortality. While common around the coast, the main concentrations of birds are in south-west Donegal – near the fishing port of Killybegs, north-west Mayo, south-west Kerry and Cork, south Wexford and Waterford, Dublin Bay, Strangford Lough and the north Antrim coast. Some Irish birds disperse to Scotland, England and Wales after the breeding season, while others move to Ireland – mainly from Britain but also from northern Europe.

See 'Gull-type Birds' p.163

ADULT

Great Black-backed Gull

Larus marinus

Droimneach mór

REALTIVELY COMMON RESIDENT. WINTER VISITOR (AUGUST–APRIL)

64–78 CM

This is the largest of our gulls and can be confused with the somewhat similar lesser black-backed gull (p.164). However, the great black-back has a black, not slate-grey, back and mantle. Also, it has flesh-coloured or whitish, not yellow, legs. It is the most maritime, and least numerous, of all Irish breeding gulls. At their breeding colonies, some black-backs will frequently snatch and eat other seabirds and their eggs. They are omnivorous feeders, often scavenging offal from fishing boats and feeding on rubbish dumps. They occur scattered around the coastline, breeding in small colonies (usually comprising less than 50 pairs) on islands, rocks and stacks. Numbers were low at the turn of the century but today there are 2,312 breeding pairs, including 71 in Northern Ireland. Most Irish-bred birds are sedentary, but some travel overseas to France, Spain and Portugal. Some Icelandic birds winter in Ireland, as evidenced by the recovery of ringed birds and observations of passage birds off the north and west coasts. During winter some considerably large flocks can be seen in estuaries and on coastal loughs.

See 'Gull-type Birds' p.163

ADULT

Kittiwake

Rissa tridactyla
Saidhbhéar
COMMON BREEDER (MARCH–OCTOBER)
38–40 CM

The kittiwake is the most pelagic of our gulls, spending half the year on the open sea, feeding and sleeping there. In the spring, kittiwakes come to islands and coastal cliffs to breed. Smaller than the common gull (p.135), the kittiwake has pale grey upper parts with diagnostic black wing tips. The bill is greenish-yellow and the legs are short and black with longer claws than other gulls, an adaptation to cliff nesting. At the breeding colonies kittiwakes are very noisy, constantly calling "kitti-ee-wayke", from which their name is derived. In flight they are buoyant and often plunge-dive for food, which is mostly small fish, marine worms, crustacea and fish offal. They depart their nesting colonies at the end of July or early August. There are 46,234 breeding pairs, including 13,060 in Northern Ireland. They are most numerous in Cos. Donegal, Kerry, Clare and Antrim. Birds ringed in Irish colonies have been recovered from a wide range of countries, including Greenland. Many foreign ringed birds, especially from Britain and France, have been found here.

See 'Gull-type Birds' p.163

ADULT
SUMMER

JUVENILE

TERNS & SMALLER GULLS

Terns – sandwich (p.170), roseate (p.171), common (p.172), Arctic (p.173) and little (p.174)
• migratory and mainly coastal
• slim bodies, short legs, narrow wings and deeply forked tails
• black caps contrasting with pale grey-and-white plumage in summer
• hover and plunge-dive for fish in shallow water
• nest on the ground, usually colonially; sensitive to disturbance
• shrill, rather harsh, "kee-ya" and/or "kier-ik" calls
• rarely walk away from the nesting area

The smaller gulls – black-headed (p.134), common (p.135), little (p.162) and Mediterranean (p.162)
• resident birds; widespread inland as well as on the coast
• plumpish bodies, medium long legs, and broad, rounded tails
• feed on the ground, or by hawking for insects
• nest on the ground, in marsh vegetation, and occasionally on trees
• squealing or scolding "kya" or "ker" calls
• walk readily and, with the exception of the little gull, often follow the plough

Sandwich Tern

Sterna sandvicensis

Geabhróg scothdhubh

LOCAL SUMMER VISITOR (MARCH–SEPTEMBER)

36–41 CM

The largest and the most gull-like of the Irish terns, the sandwich tern is easily identified by its large size and less deeply forked tail. It is also whiter than the Arctic and common terns. Its bill is black with a yellow tip; the black feathers at the back of the head are sometimes raised like a shaggy crest when the bird is on the ground in the breeding colony and in an excited state. Like the roseate tern (opposite), its flight call – a loud grating "kirrick" – is diagnostic and frequently heard in March and April, when the first birds return to Irish waters from their South African wintering grounds. Compared to other terns, sandwich terns usually dive deeper, and from a greater height, for sand eels and herring sprat. There are 3,716 pairs, including 1,954 in Northern Ireland, breeding in densely packed coastal colonies, often mixed with black-headed gulls, which act as benign protectors. The colonies are built on grassy and low rocky islands, shingle banks or in sand dunes. There is one inland colony of 21 pairs (2002) in Lower Lough Erne, Co. Fermanagh. The largest colony is at Lady's Island Lake, Co. Wexford, with 1,252 pairs in 2003.

See 'Terns & Smaller Gulls' p.163

ADULT SUMMER

ADULT SUMMER

Roseate Tern

Sterna dougallii
Geabhróg rósach
UNCOMMON LOCAL VISITOR (MAY–SEPTEMBER)
33–38 CM

ADULT
SUMMER

The roseate tern is the second rarest tern
in Ireland after the little tern (p.174),
with only 736 breeding pairs in 2003, including
712 pairs in two main coastal colonies. It is an Irish
speciality, as virtually the entire north-west European
population breeds here. The best places to see the roseate tern
are inshore coastal waters off Skerries, Loughshinny and Rush in north
Co. Dublin, where birds from the Rockabill colony (restricted access) may
be seen flying and fishing from May to July, and at Lady's Island Lake, some
6 km south-west of Rosslare Harbour (access to the colony is also
restricted). In flight the roseate tern is much whiter, with longer tail
streamers than the Arctic or common terns. Roseate wingbeats are also
shallower and faster, resembling the flight of a peregrine falcon. The
diagnostic identification characteristics are the flight calls – a long, rasping
"aak" and a happier, more gentle "chu-ick". The bill becomes increasingly
red during the breeding season, and the roseate tinge to the breast is
sometimes difficult to see. These seabirds are the last of our terns to arrive
in mid-May from their West African wintering grounds. Before departing
south in August and September, large numbers roost on Sandymount
Strand, Dublin Bay, and on Maiden Rock, Dalkey, Co. Dublin.
See 'Terns & Smaller Gulls' p.163

ADULT SUMMER

Common Tern

Sterna hirundo
Geabhróg
SUMMER VISITOR (APRIL–SEPTEMBER)
31–35 CM

Of the five Irish breeding terns, the
common tern is the most widely
distributed and most likely to be
seen. It occurs mainly in small breeding
colonies, of usually less than 100 pairs, on sand
dunes, shingle banks and rocky islands around
the coast, with concentrations in Cos. Galway and
Down. Terns have a graceful and buoyant flight, and
are generally seen within 8 km of their breeding colonies
while out on feeding missions. Nicknamed "sea swallows", they
have forked tails and swallow-like tail streamers. There are 4,189 breeding
pairs, including 1,704 in Northern Ireland, and are more likely to be
encountered than the Arctic tern in some of the inland lakes, although
numbers have decreased in recent years. Common terns have a long, grating
call, "kree-err", similar to that of the Arctic tern. They can sometimes be
very aggressive in their breeding colonies, dive-bombing human intruders
and drawing blood from the scalp by hitting it with their sharply pointed
bills. Birds arrive back in Ireland in early May from their West and South
African wintering grounds. Large numbers roost in Dublin Bay prior to
migration southwards. Most terns depart by early October.

See 'Terns & Smaller Gulls' p.169

SUMMER

SUMMER

Arctic Tern

Sterna paradisaea

Geabhróg Artach

SUMMER VISITOR (APRIL–SEPTEMBER)

33–35 CM

The best way to distinguish the Arctic tern from the common tern (opposite) is at close range. The blood-red bill of the Arctic tern has no black tip, whereas the bill of the common tern is pale orange with a black tip. Also, when standing on the ground close to the common tern, the legs of the Arctic are noticeably shorter. Finally, the Arctic tern has more grey on the neck and the upper parts. Arctic terns, like all other terns, nest colonially on rocky marine islands, shingle and sand banks, and sometimes opportunistically in waste ground or on floating rafts. They are often found in mixed breeding colonies with common terns. Some 3,502 pairs, including 767 in Northern Ireland, are widely scattered in a restricted number of colonies, with concentrations on islands and other coastal sites in Cos. Cork, Galway, Mayo, Donegal, Down and Dublin. The Arctic tern is more maritime in its choice of nesting areas than the common tern, and only 2 per cent of the population breed at inland freshwater sites as opposed to 17 per cent for the latter. The Arctic tern is one of the world's greatest bird migrants, with some individuals travelling up to 12,500 km each year. Irish birds probably winter with British birds in the Antarctic, south of the Cape of Good Hope.

See 'Terns & Smaller Gulls' p. 169

ADULT WINTER

SUMMER

Little Tern

Sterna albifrons
Geabhróg bheag
SCARCE LOCAL SUMMER VISITOR (MAY–AUGUST)
22–24 CM

The little tern is diminutive in size and has rapid wingbeats. It hovers longer than other terns before plunging into the sea. Close up, the bill is yellow with a black tip, while the forehead is white. The call is diagnostic – a constant, high-pitched, chattering "kirii-kirii-kirri". They are often seen close to the shore, in ones or twos, in the vicinity of their breeding colonies. In early May, when they return to Ireland from their west African wintering grounds, they sometimes occur in small groups, feeding together and roosting on sandy shores. The little tern is the rarest breeding tern in Ireland, with only 206 pairs scattered in small colonies on sand and shingle beaches, small shingly islands, and on some grassy-topped islands. They occur mainly on the east coast, between Cos. Meath and Wexford. The largest colony in Ireland is at Kilcoole, Co. Wicklow, where 81 pairs nested in 2003. On the west coast they are found in western Galway, Mayo and Donegal. Although fewer in breeding numbers than the roseate tern (p.171), they are not such an Irish speciality since the European population is relatively large, unlike that of the roseate. Breeding on sandy and pebbly beaches, the little tern is often subjected to human disturbance, which affects their breeding success.

See 'Terns & Smaller Gulls' p.169

JUVENILE

ADULT SUMMER

Guillemot

Uria aalge

Foracha

Common resident. At breeding colonies (March–July)
38–41 cm

The guillemot is a marine species spending most of its time in offshore and coastal waters, only arriving at the breeding colonies in February or March. It is distinguished from the somewhat similar razorbill (p.176), with which it often mixes, by its brown, not black, upper parts and a slender, pointed bill. A small proportion of birds are "bridled" with a narrow, white eye ring and line extending backwards from the eye. A total of 229,722 individuals, including 98,546 in Northern Ireland, were counted during the *Seabird 2000* survey. In their breeding colonies on islands and some coastal cliffs, the birds are packed densely together on flat ledges on steep cliff faces or on flat-topped sea stacks. These colonies are bustling with activity – comings and goings, continual jostling and pecking, and, above all, the raucous and noisy calling of a long, harsh "arrr" in a sort of growling chorus. No nests are made. However, the large eggs do not roll off the rock because of their pear shape. By the end of July–early August, the birds depart for offshore waters. In winter plumage they look quite different, with much more white on their neck and head, and can be confused with long-tailed ducks and razorbills. There are about 150,000 guillemots breeding in colonies scattered around coastal cliffs and on offshore islands.

ADULT
SUMMER
BRIDLED

ADULT
SUMMER

ADULT WINTER

Razorbill

Alca torda

Crosán

COMMON RESIDENT

AT BREEDING COLONIES (MARCH–JULY)

37–39 CM

ADULT
WINTER

The razorbill is another marine bird spending much of the year in offshore and coastal waters. The breeding colonies are occupied from March onwards, when the birds converge and pack on to ledges and under boulders to breed. A laterally compressed heavy bill with a conspicuous white line crossing it near the tip – along with black, not brown, upper parts – distinguishes the razorbill from the guillemot (p.175). Also, the razorbill's body is more compressed than the guillemot's. Both species are equally raucous in their breeding colonies. When swimming underwater, to a maximum depth of 7 m, razorbills use their stubby wings as paddles. It is quite common to see tight groups, or their "rafts", in the water close to their breeding cliffs. Razorbills have a preference for nesting away from the flat ledges favoured by the guillemots, and seek habitats with more boulders. A single egg is laid, the shape of which, like that of the guillemot, is pear-like. A total of 50,064 individuals, including 24,084 in Northern Ireland, were counted during the *Seabird 2000* survey. They breed in several island and coastal cliff colonies. Young razorbills ringed on the Saltee Islands, Co. Wexford, have been recovered in the Irish Sea, on the south coast, off Devon and Cornwall, off Iberia, in the western Mediterranean, and off north-west Africa.

ADULT SUMMER

Black Guillemot

Cepphus grylle

Foracha dhubh

LOCAL RESIDENT, AT BREEDING COLONIES (APRIL–AUGUST)

30–32 CM

ADULT WINTER

During the summer, no other bird can be mistaken for this all sooty-black auk with a conspicuous white wing patch and bright red feet. In winter it looks as if it were another species, donning a whitish-grey plumage while retaining its diagnostic white wing patch. Black guillemots do not disperse far from the coastline; so, unlike the other auks, they can frequently be seen from the mainland during the winter. They usually return to their island or coastal cliff in April, when small groups of up to 30 birds gather and perform courtship displays by pivoting around each other with their bills open, revealing bright red mouths, and calling a long-drawn-out and shrill "peeeee". A total of 4,541 individuals, including 1,174 in Northern Ireland, were counted during the *Seabird 2000* survey. They breed in 14 coastal counties, usually in small numbers at each location. Most breed in Cos. Donegal, Mayo and Antrim. Their breeding sites, which have no nesting material, are hidden in crevices or behind boulders, and even in man-made structures such as pier walls. Two eggs are laid; the other three auks only manage one. Black guillemots are very sedentary, seldom moving far from their natal area.

ADULT SUMMER

Puffin

Fratercula arctica

Puifín

COMMON LOCAL SUMMER VISITOR (APRIL–NOVEMBER), AT BREEDING COLONIES
(MARCH–AUGUST)

26–29 CM

The puffin is instantly recognised during the breeding season by its large, triangular, brightly-coloured bill and orange feet. In August, after the birds evacuate their breeding colonies, parts of the bill are shed and the red parts become dull yellow. Like the other three common auks, our puffins spend much of the year in the open Atlantic, anywhere from Newfoundland and Greenland to the Canary Islands, and even in the Mediterranean Sea near Sardinia. Puffins appear at their breeding colonies in March and remain there until August. Some 21,251 individuals, including 1,610 in Northern Ireland, were counted during the *Seabird 2000* survey. They breed in relatively few island colonies and on a few coastal cliff sites. Colonies occur in Cos. Dublin, Wexford, Cork, Kerry, Clare, Mayo, Donegal and Antrim. Puffins nest in underground tunnels, either taken over from rabbits or excavated with their massive bills. Standing outside their burrows, or in "rafts" on the water below, puffins are amongst the most striking of all birds. While many people claim that the numbers are drastically declining, there is little overall evidence to support a decline in Ireland and Britain, as shown by the special seabird surveys made in 1969–70 and 1985–87.

ADULT
SUMMER

ADULT WINTER

Rock Dove

Columba livia

Colm aille

LOCAL RESIDENT

31–34 CM

The rock dove is distinguished from the much larger wood pigeon (p.45) and stock dove (p.44) by its white rump, two pronounced black wing bars and a paler back. Rock doves are the ancestors of the racing pigeons and feral pigeons found in towns. Many of these descendants have interbred with the pure ancestral stock, and the resultant hybrids have replaced the pure-bred rock doves in the wild in many areas. The true, and probably genetically uncontaminated, rock doves are found only in the remote northern, western and southern coastal areas, far away from any possible intermingling with racing or feral pigeons. Rock doves nest in sea caves and coastal cliffs. In the autumn they gather in small flocks to feed on seeds and grain. Their flight is low, swift and dashing. They rarely perch on trees, preferring to stay on the ground. They are widespread along the west coast and the best place to see them is on the marine islands. They also occur in many inland areas in the north-eastern and eastern parts of Ireland, but these birds are likely to be genetically impure. An unknown number breed.

ADULT

ADULT

Rock Pipit

Anthus petrosus
Riabhog chladaigh
COMMON RESIDENT
16.5–17 CM

ADULT

The rock pipit is a small, grey-brown pipit found almost exclusively on or near the shoreline. It is distinguished from the meadow pipit (p.55) by dark-brown legs, grey outer tail feathers and a generally darker, less streaked plumage. Its "tsip" call is very similar to that of the meadow pipit. Spending virtually the whole year along rocky shores, especially where banks of seaweed are thrown up on small sandy beaches, they are constantly busy, foraging and chasing small flies and sandhoppers. They nest in holes or clefts in low cliffs, and are frequently used by cuckoos as foster parents. They are widely distributed, with about 12,500 pairs breeding around the coast and on offshore islands, but are noticeably absent from the long sandy shores in north Co. Louth, north Co. Wicklow and east Co. Wexford, as well as from areas with steep cliffs. Rock pipits are sedentary, with little or no movement of birds, apart from a little post-natal dispersal of juveniles. There is limited evidence of a few immigrants, possibly from Scandinavia, in the autumn.

Wheatear

Oenanthe oenanthe

Clochrán

<small>COMMON SUMMER VISITOR (MARCH–OCTOBER)</small>

14.5–15.5 CM

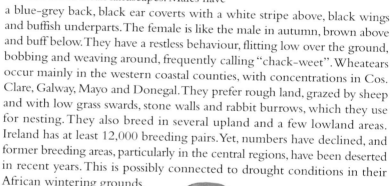

ADULT
FEMALE

The wheatear is one of the most conspicuous birds seen along the western seaboard and the east coast in March and April, when they arrive back from their African wintering grounds. The white rump and base of the tail distinguish male and female wheatears from all other common land birds found in these often bleak landscapes. Males have a blue-grey back, black ear coverts with a white stripe above, black wings and buffish underparts. The female is like the male in autumn, brown above and buff below. They have a restless behaviour, flitting low over the ground, bobbing and weaving around, frequently calling "chack-weet". Wheatears occur mainly in the western coastal counties, with concentrations in Cos. Clare, Galway, Mayo and Donegal. They prefer rough land, grazed by sheep and with low grass swards, stone walls and rabbit burrows, which they use for nesting. They also breed in several upland and a few lowland areas. Ireland has at least 12,000 breeding pairs. Yet, numbers have declined, and former breeding areas, particularly in the central regions, have been deserted in recent years. This is possibly connected to drought conditions in their African wintering grounds.

See 'Chats' p. 98

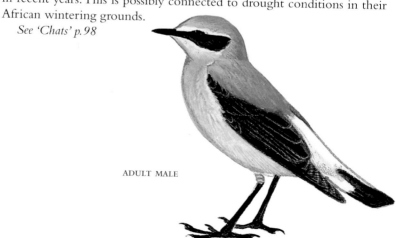

ADULT MALE

Chough

Pyrrhocorax pyrrhocorax
Cág cosdearg
UNCOMMON LOCAL RESIDENT
39–40 CM

ADULT

The chough is an Irish speciality as its population is relatively large and healthy, while there are many fewer birds in Britain, with some evidence to suggest a contraction of their breeding range there. Choughs have a glossy, black plumage and a long, curved, red bill and legs. They have a characteristic buoyant and acrobatic flight, with the widely separated primary feathers spread out like fingers when soaring. Their call is an unmistakable "kweeaw". They are very sociable, especially after the breeding season, when flocks of up to 100 birds can be seen stabbing their powerful bills into close-cropped turf in search of small insect larvae, along cliff tops or on lowland grassland, and especially on machair grassland behind sand dunes. Breeding birds occur either in single pairs or sometimes in small colonies on the west and northern coasts and islands, where they nest in caves and often in old buildings. They breed at about three years old, with an average life expectancy of about ten years. Winter flocks will only wander locally.

County	1992 Survey			2002/03 Survey			% Status Change (based on totals)
	Pairs[a]	Flock birds	Total	Pairs[a]	Flock birds	Total	
Wexford	1–8	15	31	0–3	5	11	–65
Waterford	4–49	93	191	9–50	63	163	–15
Cork	67–282	292	856	114–259	273	791	–8
Kerry	53–315	122	752	121–263	242	768	+2
Clare	16–28	17	73	9–29	21	79	+8
Galway	20–38	28	104	14–20	9	49	–53
Mayo	23–65	66	196	26–60★	60★	180★	–8
Sligo/Leitrim	7–18	22	58	12–15	29	59	+2
Donegal	28–101	164	366	74–129	68	326	–11
TOTAL	**906**	**821**	**2,633**	**828**	**770**	**2,426**	**–8**

[a] = figures for pairs include confirmed, probable and possible breeders
★ = projected figures
Source: *Wings* (Quarterly magazine of BirdWatch Ireland) 30 p.6
Table: Number of Choughs in Ireland 1992 and 2002/03

Tree Sparrow

Passer montanus
Gealbhan crainn
LOCAL RESIDENT
14 CM

JUVENILE

Distinguished from the male house sparrow (p.22) by a chocolate-brown crown and a black patch on white cheeks, male and female tree sparrows have the same plumage. Their flight call is a distinctive and harsh "teck-teck". Tree sparrows are easily overlooked and often mistaken as house sparrows. In Ireland they are less closely associated with man than in Britain. Numbers fluctuate; in the 1950s the species became extinct in Ireland but recovered in the 1960s, with an estimated current population of up to 1,500 pairs. The tree sparrow has a coastal distribution in western Ireland, with birds breeding on islands and in ruined and derelict coastal buildings. It is much more abundant inland, breeding in small colonies in eastern and north-eastern Ireland – the main Irish breeding stronghold is in the Lough Neagh Basin, Co. Antrim. Meath, Louth and Dublin are also important counties. They also breed in other counties, with south Co. Wexford accounting for a good population. During the winter, tree sparrows flock together to feed on fallen grain; winter flocks of up to 400 birds have been seen at Comber, Co. Down, while up to 100 birds have been reported in Cos. Louth, Meath, Donegal, Kerry and Wexford.

See 'Sparrows' p.21

ADULT

Twite

Carduelis flavirostris
Gleoiseach sléibhe
UNCOMMON LOCAL RESIDENT, DECLINING
14 CM

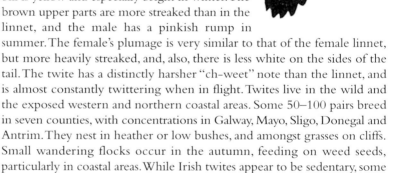

ADULT FEMALE
SUMMER

The twite is a small brown finch, somewhat similar in size and appearance to the linnet (p.103) and the redpoll (p.86). All three sometimes occur in mixed flocks in coastal areas. The twite differs, however, by having a more slender body and a long, forked tail. Close up, its bill is yellow and especially bright in winter. The brown upper parts are more streaked than in the linnet, and the male has a pinkish rump in summer. The female's plumage is very similar to that of the female linnet, but more heavily streaked, and, also, there is less white on the sides of the tail. The twite has a distinctly harsher "ch-weet" note than the linnet, and is almost constantly twittering when in flight. Twites live in the wild and the exposed western and northern coastal areas. Some 50–100 pairs breed in seven counties, with concentrations in Galway, Mayo, Sligo, Donegal and Antrim. They nest in heather or low bushes, and amongst grasses on cliffs. Small wandering flocks occur in the autumn, feeding on weed seeds, particularly in coastal areas. While Irish twites appear to be sedentary, some move south from Scotland to winter here.

See 'Finches' p.21

ADULT MALE SUMMER

Little Egret

Egretta garzetta
Éigrit callaigh
RESIDENT. RARE BREEDER, INCREASING
43–51 CM

ADULT
SUMMER

A small, bright, white heron with a long thin neck, black bill and legs with yellow feet. During summer adults develop two long (16 cm) drooping crest feathers, coveted by the 19th-century plumage trade, which led to population declines throughout Europe, though numbers recovered in the next century following the ban on feather trade. Rarely seen away from fresh water, marshes, lagoons and the edges of lakes and rivers. Formerly a scarce visitor to southern coastal counties, the first Irish record was in 1940, followed by 13 more between 1957–65. Most frequently seen between April and October, with the largest numbers from early May, as migrants "overshoot" their extensive French breeding sites. An Irish breeder now, following an increase in number of visitors, plus extended stays, first noted during the mid-1990s, with upwards of 60 wintering birds. First bred in 1997, when 12 pairs nested at one site, Co. Cork. Since then, another three sites have been established in Cos. Cork and Waterford. The total Irish breeding population in 1999 was 32 pairs; 55 pairs in 2001 and 122+ pairs in 2003. Beech trees, followed by oak, in mature woodland are the most favoured nesting sites. Colonies are located close to estuarine habitats, usually within 10 km. Egrets feed by wading through shallow waters, darting their long bills into the water to spear small fish and invertebrates. Often seen running around madly in shallow water in pursuit of prey. Increasingly seen in other coastal countries outside the breeding season. Breeding population will increase and spread.

ADULT

JUVENILE

Pink-footed Goose

Anser brachyrhynchus

Gé ghobgherarr

SCARCE WINTER VISITOR. (OCTOBER–APRIL)

60–75 CM

Distinguished from other grey geese by a dark head and neck, markedly contrasting with the pale-grey upper parts. The bill is small, pink and black. The feet are pink. Annual visitors, generally to coastal counties, occurring in small numbers, usually up to five birds; flocks of over 20 are unusual. It is the most numerous (215,000 birds) wintering goose in Britain, and most of our visitors are probably overspills from the Scottish wintering population – five ringed there during the autumn have been shot in Ireland. Other birds may come directly from the Icelandic/Greenland breeding population – 12 recoveries of summer-ringed Icelandic birds are recorded in Ireland. Two pink-footed geese ringed on the North Slob, Co. Wexford, during the winters of 1986 and 1987 were shot three winters later, in Norfolk and Scotland. During 1996–2000, a total of 820 were recorded in Ireland at favourite coastal haunts: Lough Swilly – Blanket Nook – Inch Lough, and Dunfanaghy, Co. Donegal; Lough Beg, Co. Derry; Quoile Pondage, Co. Down; Braganstown/Stabannon, Lurgangreen and Commons Road, Co. Louth and North Slob, Co. Wexford. Inland records frequently noted at Rahasane Turlough, Co. Galway, and at the river Little Brosna Callows, Co. Offaly.

See 'Geese' p.120

ADULT

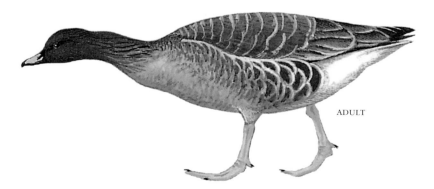

ADULT

Light-bellied Brent Goose

Branta bernicla hrota

Cadhan

WINTER VISITOR (SEPTEMBER–MAY)

56–61 CM

The brent goose is the smallest and darkest of the "black geese", with a black head, breast and back. The light-bellied race is the one that winters in Ireland; it has pale underparts contrasting with the darker upper parts. The dark-bellied race has a dark grey-brown belly and is a scarce winter visitor. The upper- and under-tail coverts are pure white and adults have a small, whitish patch on the upper neck. As many as 20,900 birds, from arctic Canada, were counted in October 2002, in the larger estuaries, bays, lagoons and coastal marshes, after the first birds arrived back in Ireland at the end of August. Like other geese, they are very gregarious and sociable. Largest numbers occur in Cos. Antrim, Dublin, Wexford, Waterford, Kerry, Sligo and Donegal. They feed by walking along the tideline or across mudflats, picking up vegetation. They also "upend" to pluck deeper seaweed and the eel grass *Zostera* from the bottom. Birds frequently graze on sports fields close to North Bull Island, Dublin Bay, while others feed on the improved grasslands on the Wexford Slobs. Their regular call is a throaty "rroonk". They generally fly in long, straggly, undulating lines.

See 'Geese' p.120

ADULT

Shelduck

Tadorna tadorna

Seil-lacha

FAIRLY COMMON RESIDENT

WINTER VISITOR (OCTOBER–MARCH)

58–67 CM

JUVENILE

This is a large, goose-like duck, exotic-looking in its boldly contrasting black, white and chestnut plumage. The male and female are similarly coloured with a greenish-black head and neck, and a white body with a broad chestnut band around its forepart. The white forewings, back and tail are conspicuous in flight. The bill is red, and in the male it has a large knob at the base. They are widely scattered in low-lying coastal areas, where there are muddy shores, estuaries, bays and sand dunes. About 1,100 pairs breed in Ireland, setting up base wherever they find good nesting sites such as rabbit burrows and an abundant supply of invertebrates, particularly the small Hydrobia snail of the mudflats. Some birds also breed inland, in lower Lough Erne, Co. Fermanagh; Lough Neagh, Co. Antrim and Poulaphouca Reservoir, Co. Wicklow. When breeding is finished in July, the adults leave their young in a creche and fly to the mass-moulting grounds in the Heligoland Bight in Germany, and to other probable sites closer to Ireland – such as Bridgewater Bay in the Bristol Channel. They start returning October onwards, and are augmented with Continental visitors to make up the wintering population.

See 'Ducks' p.120–1

ADULT SUMMER

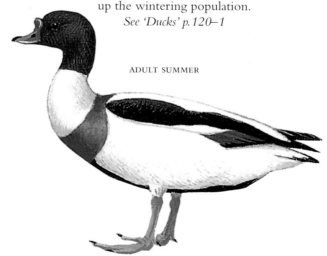

Scaup

Aythya marila

Lacha iascán

<small>LOCAL WINTER VISITOR (OCTOBER–APRIL)</small>

42–51 CM

The male scaup differs from the similar tufted duck (p.128) by having a pale-grey back, which, together with the white flanks, gives the impression of a white duck with black ends. The head, chest and tail are black. The female scaup is dark brown with a noticeable white patch at the base of the bill. In flight both sexes have a white rear-wing stripe, similar to the tufted duck's. Scaups are robust sea ducks and seem little affected by stormy conditions or harsh weather. Expert divers, they feed mainly on bivalve molluscs, particularly mussels. Scaups are found around the coast, usually in small flocks, occurring mainly at Belfast Lough, Co. Antrim; Carlingford Lough, Co. Louth; Wexford Harbour, Co. Wexford; Tralee Bay and Castlemaine Harbour, Co. Kerry; Shannon Estuary; Donegal Bay and Lough Swilly, Co. Donegal. Lough Neagh, Co. Antrim is the largest inland haunt, with upwards of 4,000 birds. About 5,000 birds winter in Ireland, mainly coming from Iceland and some from Europe. It bred in Northern Ireland in 1997 and 1999.

See 'Ducks' p. 120–1

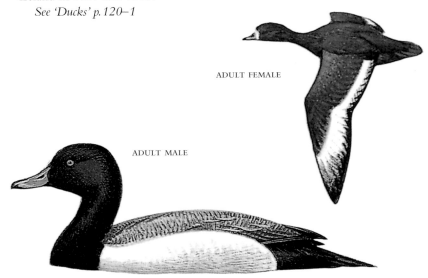

ADULT FEMALE

ADULT MALE

Wigeon

Anas penelope

Rualacha

VERY RARE BREEDER (UP TO 5 PAIRS)

COMMON WINTER VISITOR (AUGUST–APRIL)

45–51 CM

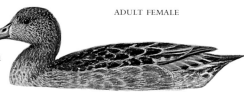

ADULT FEMALE

The drake has a chestnut head with a lighter yellow, buff forehead, greyish upper parts and a white patch on the front of the wing which is very noticeable in flight. The female is the usual rufous brown. Both sexes have a blue bill. Wigeons are gregarious; winter visitors are equally at home in estuaries and coastal loughs, turloughs, callow lands and inland freshwater lakes. They can rise almost vertically off the water and have a rapid, direct flight. The call of the drake is a very distinctive, musical whistling, "whee-oo", heard as frequently on the wing as on the water. The female has a low purring call. Wigeons are our most numerous wintering duck, with about 100,000 birds coming from Iceland, Scandinavia, north-east Russia and south-west Siberia. Wigeons occur in most coastal areas, with fewest birds north of Galway to Lough Swilly, Co. Donegal. Large flocks are found inland, grazing damp pastures in turloughs and callow lands associated with the rivers Shannon and Suck, Co. Roscommon.

See 'Ducks' p. 120–1

ADULT MALE

Pintail

Anas acuta

Biorearrach

VERY RARE BREEDER (UP TO 5 PAIRS)

WINTER VISITOR (SEPTEMBER–APRIL)

51–66 CM

The drake pintail is probably the most elegant of our ducks. It has a grey body, a chocolate-brown head and neck, with a white streak on either side of an elongated, thin neck, and a white chest. Its tail is extremely long, extending up to 19 cm, and sharply pointed. The female is a less striking brown, in keeping with the lack of brilliance of most female ducks. Such inconspicuousness protects the female from the predators when incubating the eggs. Numbers wintering in Ireland have declined in recent years, from about 7,000 to about 2,000 birds. The largest concentrations are in coastal sites: Rogerstown Estuary and North Bull, Co. Dublin; Strangford Lough, Co. Down and Tacumshin, Co. Wexford. They also occur in many inland sites, and in particular the River Shannon system and its associated callow lands and turloughs. Winter visitors originate mainly in Iceland, with fewer numbers from Russia. Pintails have bred intermittently from 1923 at Loughs Neagh and Beg, Co. Antrim, but are now very rare-breeding birds. They breed spasmodically in Co. Roscommon.

See 'Ducks' p. 120–1

ADULT
FEMALE

ADULT MALE

WADERS

Waders vary widely in size, and length of bill and legs:
• large: curlew (p.52), oystercatcher (p.43), bar-tailed (p.204) and
black-tailed godwit (p.203), whimbrel (p.205), woodcock (p.68)
• medium: lapwing (p.51), golden (p.50) and grey (p.195) plover,
redshank (p.201), greenshank (p.202), knot (p.196), snipe (p.132)
• small: ringed plover (p.194), dunlin (p.199), sanderling (p.197),
purple (p.159, common (p.133) and curlew (p.198) sandpiper,
(p.160) and little stint (p.148)

Useful clues to identification are:
• habitat and feeding method
• length and colour of legs and bill
• position of any white patches/bars on wings, rump
and/or tail
In autumn many coastal waders are young birds, which
are drabber and often browner than adults.
Adults in spring and early autumn often
show some of their breeding-season
colours.

RINGED PLOVER

OYESTERCATCHER

REDSHANK

Oystercatcher

Haematopus ostralegus

Roilleach

COMMON RESIDENT.

COMMON WINTER VISITOR (OCTOBER–MARCH)

40–45 CM

ADULT
SUMMER

The most conspicuous of all our wading birds, the oystercatcher is large-bodied, with a long orange bill, pink legs and black-and-white plumage. Both sexes are similar. They are noisy and wary birds, often calling their loud note – a shrill "kleep-kleep" or an acute "pic-pic". During spring courtship they have a "piping display", when several birds run around together in a frenzied fashion, with their heads and bills pointed down, their shoulders lifted, and making a piping trill with their bills open. The ceremonies are attended by up to 12 birds and go on for several minutes. The oystercatcher is widespread as a breeding bird, nesting on, or near, shingly shores or amongst rocks and grasses. The size of the breeding population is about 3,000–4,000 pairs, with the greatest numbers along the west, north-west and north-eastern coastlines. A small number breed inland but it is not such a common habit as in Britain, where coastal pressures have driven the birds inland. About 70,000 wintering birds occur mainly in sandy estuaries, bays and loughs, with a good scattering of birds around the whole coastline. They are most abundant in places where there is a good supply of cockles and mussels.

See 'Waders' p.192

ADULT SUMMER

Ringed Plover

Charadrius hiaticula

Feadóg chladaigh

FAIRLY COMMON RESIDENT

WINTER VISITOR (SEPTEMBER–APRIL)

18–20 CM

ADULT SUMMER

The ringed plover is a small, plumpish wader with a marked black-and-white head pattern, a broad black band across its white chest, orange legs and sandy-brown upper parts. It has the characteristic plover behaviour of standing still and rigid, running forwards with brief pauses, bending forwards to pick up a small insect, standing still again and running forwards. When standing still, their brown upper parts and broken head pattern provide excellent camouflage in their usually sandy or pebbly habitats. Young ringed plovers have an incomplete chest band and scaly brown upper parts. In flight, a prominent white wing bar is exposed. If a breeding bird is disturbed, it may distract the human or animal predator by an "injury-feigning" display in which the bird drags its body along the ground, with its tail spread out and one wing extended and flapping as if it were injured. This behaviour has fooled many a human. The estimated 1,250 pairs of breeding birds are distributed widely around the coast, with the highest concentrations in sandy and shingly areas. The greatest numbers occur in the north-west. Many birds from Greenland, Iceland and north Europe migrate through Ireland while passing south, with others wintering here, bringing the population up to some 5,000–10,000 birds.

See 'Waders' p.192

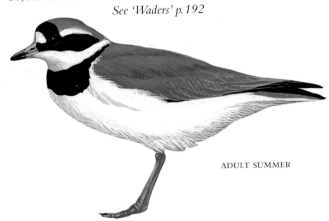

ADULT SUMMER

Grey Plover

Pluvialis squatarola

Feadóg ghlas

WINTER VISITOR, RECENT INCREASE (AUGUST–MAY)

27–30 CM

Grey plovers seem to be the least sociable of waders, seldom occurring in medium or large flocks and preferring to space themselves out in small groups along open beaches, sandy areas and some muddy shores. They are somewhat similar to the knot (p.196) and golden plover (p.50), but can be distinguished by their conspicuous black "armpits", only visible when they are in flight, and their white rump. Their call is diagnostic, a sometimes plaintive "hee-oo-ee", which will, as with so many other bird calls, be the first indication that grey plovers are in the area. In winter their upper parts are brownish-grey and the underparts, white. On the ground the birds stand much more upright than knot and have a shorter bill. Their general behaviour is typical of plovers. Like the knot, they are concentrated in the large muddier estuaries, bays and loughs. Up to 5,000 birds from Siberia winter mainly in Strangford Lough, Co. Down; Dundrum Bay, Co. Down; North Bull, Dublin; Wexford Harbour; Cork Harbour; Tralee Bay, Co. Kerry; Shannon Estuary and Killala Bay, Co. Mayo. There are smaller numbers scattered around the coast.

See 'Waders' p.192

ADULT
WINTER

ADULT WINTER MALE

Knot

Calidris canutus

Cnota

WINTER VISITOR (OCTOBER–MARCH)

PASSAGE MIGRANT (AUGUST–SEPTEMBER)

23–25 CM

ADULT
WINTER

The knot is a stockily built, medium-sized wader which in winter plumage is an undistinguished white and grey. Its upper parts are ash-grey while the underparts are whiter, streaked with black. The bill is short and black, and the legs are olive-green. Some of the first knots returning in late July – from their high arctic breeding grounds in Canada and Greenland – will still retain their summer plumage of mottled, black-chestnut upper parts, as well as their russet head and underparts. During the winter they feed and fly in dense packs, preferring muddy estuaries, especially on the east coast. They are not very noisy and their flight call is a soft "twit-twit-twit". Knots are relatively fewer in Ireland than in Britain, and there is evidence to show that their wintering numbers have decreased in the past 30 years to about 25,000 birds today. Their main haunts are in the large muddy estuaries and bays at Strangford Lough, Co. Down; Boyne Estuary, Co. Meath; Dundrum Bay, Co. Down; North Bull, Dublin and Wexford Harbour. Smaller numbers are at Tralee Bay, Co. Kerry; Shannon Estuary; and Lough Foyle, Co. Derry.

See 'Waders' p. 192

ADULT WINTER

Sanderling

Calidris alba
Luathrán
WINTER VISITOR (AUGUST–APRIL)
PASSAGE MIGRANT (JULY AND AUGUST)
20–21 CM

A small busy wader, the sanderling is immediately identified by its clockwork-like behaviour of continual running backwards and forwards, along the tideline of a sandy shore in search of sandhoppers and other small insects. In the autumn, on arrival from their Greenland and possibly Siberian breeding grounds, their head, upper parts and breast are a chestnut-brown speckled with black. Their belly is a pure white. In winter plumage they are the whitest of all our small waders – with a white head and white underparts, while their upper parts turn pale-grey, with a conspicuous black shoulder mark. Small groups of sanderling are relatively tame, allowing close approach. Their characteristic note is "twick-twick", which they call when disturbed, but also when feeding. While a large number of birds probably pass through Ireland in the autumn, on migration to Africa, about 4,000 birds stay with us to winter here. They are mostly found on open sandy beaches and in some estuaries, especially on the west coast but also in Cos. Meath, Dublin, Wexford, Waterford and Cork. There is a pronounced spring passage northwards along the west coast, especially in Co. Mayo, with flocks of up to 400 birds being recorded.

See 'Waders' p.192

ADULT WINTER

ADULT WINTER

Curlew Sandpiper

Calidris ferruginea
Gobadán crotaigh
UNCOMMON PASSAGE MIGRANT IN VARIABLE NUMBERS
(OCTOBER–APRIL)
18–19 CM

The curlew sandpiper superficially resembles a dunlin, a fellow traveller, but in flight has a conspicuous white rump, whereas the dunlin has a dark brown centre to its rump. The former has longer legs, a cleaner cut to the bodyline and a more upright stance. The bill is longer, thinner and, importantly, down-curved (hence the name). Easy to overlook, but once identified, others begin to appear in a flock of dunlin or other waders. Formerly thought uncommon, probably due to recognition difficulties and paucity of birdwatchers. Over 300 were recorded in the year 2000, mostly in small numbers and principally during autumn migration. Co. Wexford is one of the best areas to see them, especially at Tacumshin, The Cull and Rosslare Back Strand. Other good locations are Swords, Rogerstown and Baldoyle estuaries and North Bull Island, Co. Dublin, and in Co. Wicklow at Kilcoole. Although mostly seen on the east and southern coasts, large numbers sometimes appear in Co. Kerry at Blennerville, Blackrock Strand and Carahane Sands.

ADULT
WINTER

See 'Waders' p. 192

Little Stint

Calidris minuta
Gobadáinín beag
UNCOMMON PASSAGE MIGRANT (AUGUST–OCTOBER)
12–14 CM

WINTER

This other autumn migrant, and often a fellow traveller of the Curlew Sandpiper, is the smallest common wader seen in Ireland. It is an uncommon passage migrant occurring in variable numbers, totalling about 300–400 in a good year. One-fifth smaller than the dunlin, it has a straight and shorter bill. Estuaries and bays along the east and southern coasts are its favoured locations.

See 'Waders' p. 192

Dunlin

Calidris alpina

Breacóg

SCARCE LOCAL BREEDER, RECENT DECLINE

COMMON WINTER VISITOR (AUGUST–APRIL)

16–20 CM

WINTER

The commonest wintering wader, the dunlin is found principally around the coast and occasionally in turloughs and in the Shannon callow lands. Dunlin appear in the major muddy estuaries, lagoons, bays and loughs. When feeding they often follow the tideline, probing the mud busily for small invertebrates. At high tide, they form densely packed roosts. In the air, large flocks perform aerial gyrations, with synchronised movements between the birds. Dunlin are small, with a down-curved black bill. In winter plumage they have streaked, brownish-grey upper parts and white underparts. In flight they have a white wing bar and wide brighter sides to the tail. Their contact call is a short, sharp "dzee", which is often heard at night when the birds are flying overhead during spring and autumn migrations. In summer, dunlin have a large, black belly patch and warm, brown upper parts. An estimated 200–300 pairs breed in Ireland (2002), mainly in coastal areas, while there are some 120,000 wintering birds coming from Scandinavia, Russia and other northern areas.

WINTER

See 'Waders' p.192

SUMMER

Ruff

Philomachus pugnax
Rufachán
UNCOMMON PASSAGE MIGRANT (AUGUST–OCTOBER).
20–30 CM

The ruff (male) is about the size of a redshank and, in autumn, has sandy upper parts and "scaly" wings and back, a heavier body, a short, heavy bill, rounded head and long legs (grey-brown to green, to orange). It stands erect. In flight it has conspicuous white oval patches on either side of the dark tail. The reeve (female) is a smaller version of the ruff. Occurring usually in small numbers (up to 10 normally, although 120 have been seen at Tacumshin, Co. Wexford) in coastal locations – estuaries, marshes and lagoons – as well at various inland sites – turloughs and lakeshores. More are seen in Co. Wexford than in any other area, while

ADULT
FEMALE

ADULT MALE
WINTER

they are regularly reported from Cos. Louth (Dundalk Docks); Galway (Rahasane Turlough); Dublin (Swords and Rogerstown estuaries); Donegal (Lough Swilly); Kerry (Akeragh Lough, Blennerville and Carrahane); Cork (Ballycotton, the Gearagh and Clonakilty) and Loughs Neagh and Beg.
See 'Waders' p. 192

Spotted Redshank

Tringa erythropus
Cosdeargán breac
UNCOMMON PASSAGE MIGRANT MAINLY (AUGUST–OCTOBER)
29–31 CM

Visits Ireland at the same time, and at the same habitats, as the ruff; usually less than 100 records a year, but it is an increasing winter visitor, especially to the southern counties. In its late autumn and winter plumage, it looks similar to the redshank, but in flight it is distinguished by the lack of a white wing bar. The diagnostic feature, however, is the call – a strong "tchuit, tchuit, tchuit" that announces the bird's presence usually before it is seen.
See 'Waders' p. 192

ADULT
WINTER

Redshank

Tringa totanus
Cosdeargán
LOCAL BREEDER. COMMON WINTER VISITOR (JULY–APRIL)
27–29 CM

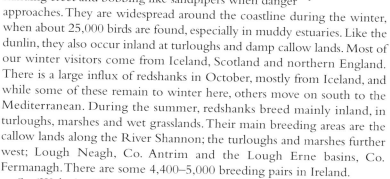

ADULT

The redshank is a conspicuous and noisy bird, with long orange-red legs, grey-brown upper parts and whitish underparts streaked with sepia. No other wader has a similar flight pattern of large, white hind edges to the wings, a white rump, and tail and legs dangling behind. When disturbed it invariably calls a musical "tleu-tu-tu" as it flies off. Redshanks are shy and nervous birds, standing erect and bobbing like sandpipers when danger approaches. They are widespread around the coastline during the winter, when about 25,000 birds are found, especially in muddy estuaries. Like the dunlin, they also occur inland at turloughs and damp callow lands. Most of our winter visitors come from Iceland, Scotland and northern England. There is a large influx of redshanks in October, mostly from Iceland, and while some of these remain to winter here, others move on south to the Mediterranean. During the summer, redshanks breed mainly inland, in turloughs, marshes and wet grasslands. Their main breeding areas are the callow lands along the River Shannon; the turloughs and marshes further west; Lough Neagh, Co. Antrim and the Lough Erne basins, Co. Fermanagh. There are some 4,400–5,000 breeding pairs in Ireland.

See 'Waders' p.192

ADULT SUMMER

Greenshank

Tringa nebularia

Laidhrin glas

PASSAGE MIGRANT AND WINTER VISITOR (JULY–APRIL)

30–33 CM

ADULT WINTER

The greenshank is somewhat similar to the redshank (p.201), but is larger and greyer, with longer, green legs, a slightly upturned black bill and, most importantly, no white on the wing. The upper parts are ash-grey, and the head, neck and underparts are white. In flight, their dark, almost black wings contrast sharply with the bright, white rump that extends up the back. Greenshanks have a loud, clear and staccato call, "tew-twe-twe", often announcing their presence before being seen. When feeding in shallow estuarine waters, they often run after small fish and shrimps, darting from side to side. Ireland is an important wintering area for the estimated 1,350 pairs breeding in Scotland. The wintering population in Ireland is about 2,000 birds. Greenshanks are well distributed around the coast, and especially abundant in muddy estuaries, bays and creeks. Although usually occurring in singles or pairs, larger numbers of up to 50 birds may be encountered in a few estuaries such as Strangford Lough, Co. Down; Carlingford Lough, Co. Louth; Dundrum Bay, Co. Down; Cork Harbour; Castlemaine Harbour and Co. Kerry; Shannon Estuary; Galway Bay; Sligo Bay; Tralee Bay; Lough Foyle, Co. Derry and Lough Swilly, Co. Donegal. Has bred at least three times at the same site in Co. Mayo.

See 'Waders' p.192

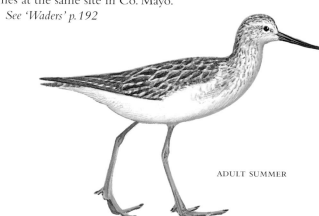

ADULT SUMMER

Black-tailed Godwit

Limosa limosa

Guilbneach earrdhubh

VERY RARE BREEDER. WINTER VISITOR (JULY–MARCH)

40–44 CM

WINTER

In flight, the black-tailed godwit is distinguished from the similar bar-tailed godwit (p.204) by a broad, white wing bar edged on either side by dark feathers, and a broad, black band at the end of its pure-white tail. Also, its legs extend further beyond the tail. The bill is straighter and less upturned than the bar-tailed godwit's. Black-tailed godwits returning from their Icelandic breeding grounds as early as the end of June are still in their extremely handsome summer plumage, with their chestnut-coloured head, neck and breast, and their white belly barred with black. Up to 8,000 birds occur during the winter, with occasional larger numbers during spring migration. They have a much more restricted coastal distribution than the bar-tailed godwit, preferring muddier, less sandy habitats. The most important area is the Little Brosna Callows. Most of the birds occur along the south coast at Clonakilty Bay and Ballymacoda Bay, Co. Cork, and Cork Harbour. In Waterford, Dungarvan Bay holds large numbers, and so do Wexford Harbour and the Shannon and Fergus estuaries. Smaller numbers occur on the east coast, from County Dublin to Dundalk Bay, Co. Louth. They are scarce on the northern and western coasts. Many hundreds also winter inland on the wet callow lands of the River Shannon. Large numbers have been recorded in the Shannon Estuary during spring migration. A few pairs breed in the Shannon callow lands.

See 'Waders' p.192

ADULT SUMMER

Bar-tailed Godwit

Limosa lapponica

Guilbneach stríocearrach

WINTER VISITOR (JULY–APRIL)

37–39 CM

ADULT WINTER

Godwits are long-legged, long-billed and upright-standing waders. They are bigger than the redshank (p.201), but smaller than the curlew (p.52). In winter the upper parts are mottled grey, with whitish underparts. They are distinguished from the similar black-tailed godwit (p.203) by the absence of a broad, white wing bar and a bold, black band on the tail. Their colouring in flight resembles the curlew's, with mottled grey upper parts, a white rump and black barring to the tail. Close up, the bar-tailed godwit has a slightly shorter and more upturned bill than the black-tailed godwit. Male birds returning early to Ireland in July – from their north Scandinavian and Russian breeding grounds – will have a rich chestnut colouring about the neck and breast. Their winter distribution is strictly coastal, with largest numbers in the big muddy and sandy estuaries, bays and lagoons, where up to 17,500 may be seen at a time, as in Dundalk Bay, Co. Louth; Lough Foyle, Co. Derry; Dublin Bay or Wexford Harbour and Slobs. They often plunge their long bills full-length into the mud to extract tasty lugworm. They will also eat shrimps, sandhoppers, small crabs and bivalve molluscs. About 17,000 winter in Ireland.

See 'Waders' p.192

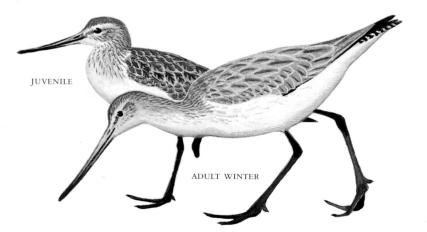

JUVENILE

ADULT WINTER

Whimbrel

Numenius phaeopus
Crotach eanaigh
PASSAGE MIGRANT (APRIL–MAY AND AUGUST–SEPTEMBER)
40–42 CM

The whimbrel resembles the curlew (p.*52*), but is smaller with a shorter bill and a black-striped head when seen close up. Its call is quite distinctive, and frequently heard when the birds are passing through Ireland on their spring and autumn migration. This call is best described as a rapid tittering of about seven whistling notes, each of equal length and intensity. Bursts of the seven notes are repeated regularly. It is easy to imitate, and birds hearing it will be attracted to the caller. Whimbrels pass through Ireland in the spring, on migration from their African wintering grounds to their Icelandic breeding grounds. They generally occur in small groups in southern and western coastal areas, preferring the rocky coastline, estuaries and salt marshes. A large number of birds also pass through central Ireland, especially through the River Shannon system and the large western lakes. Up to 3,300 birds have been reported flying over Cork Harbour during the spring migration. A few birds summer in Ireland and an increasing number, usually of singles, winter in Cork.

See 'Waders' p.192

ADULT

Short Eared Owl

Asio flammeus

Ulchabhán réisc

HAS BRED. UNCOMMON WINTER VISITOR (OCTOBER–APRIL).

62–68 CM

A long-winged owl with a dark patch on the underwing at the carpal joint, and longer winged than the short-eared owl with which it may be confused. Heavily brown-streaked, especially the chest, pale yellow-brown plumage. Flight is a "rowing" type, the wings held up in a shallow V at low speeds. It is the most diurnal of all owls in Ireland, and more often seen than the two other owls – barn and long-eared. Often perches on the ground. First recorded breeding was on the Mullet, Co. Mayo, 1932; unsuccessful. Successful breeding in Co. Galway, 1959. Single pairs nested in Cos. Kerry and Limerick in 1977, and there have been isolated breeding subsequently. Three pairs breed, Glens of Antrim, 1999, having first bred in north Ireland in 1997. Another pair bred in the Sperrins, Co. Tyrone, in 2000. Winter visitors, from Scotland, Britain – young ringed in Scotland (4), northern England (1) and Isle of Man (1) have been recovered in Ireland – and the Continent arrive in October, scattering themselves thinly throughout the country, with largest numbers reported from the east coast, especially in Co. Dublin where North Bull and Dalkey islands are favoured locations. Most frequently seen in open habitats – marshes, sand dunes and moorland.

ADULT

ADULT

Snow Bunting

Plectrophenax nivalis

Gealóg shneachta.

UNCOMMON WINTER VISITOR AND PASSAGE MIGRANT (SEPTEMBER–APRIL).
16–17 CM

ADULT
FEMALE

Identified by broad white patches on wings and tail to resemble a snowflake in flight. The female's head is grey-brown, with a brown stripe from the eye to ear-coverts. In spring the male is a striking black-and-white bird, with black back, primary wing feathers and tail feathers; the rest of the

ADULT MALE
WINTER

plumage is white. Typically high flying, uttering its unmistakable, plaintive contact call "teu". First migrants generally arrive end–September/early–October, probably from Greenland and Iceland rather than Scandinavia. Occurs generally in small numbers, but flocks of up to 20 not uncommon; occasionally flocks of 200 recorded. Wintering birds remain near the seashore, to feed principally upon seeds of grasses and weeds found on open rough ground. Often seen on coastal golf courses. Seldom observed in trees or bushes. One pair may have bred in Co. Donegal, 1977.

Lapland Bunting

Calcarius lapponicus

Gealóg Lalannach

UNCOMMON AUTUMN PASSAGE MIGRANT
(SEPTEMBER–OCTOBER) AND WINTER VISITOR
15–16 CM

ADULT FEMALE WINTER

Also a passage migrant and winter visitor, but occurs in much fewer numbers, from northern Scandinavia. Both sexes are a streaky brown, the male has some reddish brown on its nape. The call is a musical "teeleu", the note falling away at the end, and is distinct from that of the snow bunting. First migrants arrive at the end of August, some 20–30 individuals have been recorded arriving each day at Tory Island, Malin Head, Inishstrahull, Co. Donegal, and Erris Head, Co. Mayo – with numbers increasing from early September and declining October. Spends most of its time on open ground, running around more than the snow bunting.

ADULT FEMALE
SUMMER

PLACES TO VISIT

In this chapter I have selected 73 places to visit, where one can see most of the birds described in the book without too much trouble. Only the bare essentials for each have been given. Additional information can be obtained from two more detailed guides, *Where to Watch Birds in Ireland* by Clive Hutchinson (Gill & Macmillan, 1994) and *Nature Atlas of Great Britain, Ireland and the Channel Islands* (Pan/Ordnance Survey, 1989). The sites chosen have been arranged on a county basis, each county being listed alphabetically within the four provinces of Ireland. While most landowners are welcoming to naturalists and birdwatchers, it is important to respect their property and to observe the basic country code, as well as to avoid any disturbance to wildlife.

More detailed information can be obtained from two key websites:

Northern Ireland: www.ehsni.gov.uk

Republic of Ireland: www.duchas.ie

The following are useful reference web sites:

www.birdwatchireland.ie
www.birdsireland.com
www.irishbirding.com
www.rspb.org.uk/nireland
www.interknowledge.com/northern-ireland/ukibrd01.htm

ULSTER

ANTRIM

1. Rathlin Island

The best time to visit Rathlin Island is from early May to early July, when the large seabird populations are in their busiest period. The principal colonies are at the west-end cliffs, where razorbills, guillemots, black guillemots, puffins, fulmars, kittiwakes, herring and lesser and great black-backed gulls can easily be watched. Also found on Rathlin are Manx shearwaters, common and black-headed gulls (nesting on the island lakes), and eiders (nesting on the southern extension). Breeding buzzards and several pairs of peregrines and ravens are special island features. Twites have been recorded breeding on Rathlin, and so too a few pairs of whinchats. There is a regular boat service from Ballycastle during the summer, and accommodation is available on the island. Contact: Alison Hurst, RSPB Information Warden, Raithlin Island. (Tel: 028 207 63948.) For boat, contact Caledonian MacBryne, Tel: 028 207 69299.

• www.rspb.org.uk/reserves/guide/r/rathlinisland/index.asp

2. Lough Neagh: Shane's Castle Park

This park provides one of the best viewing points of Lough Neagh, especially from the castle itself. Large flocks of wildfowl may be seen in the autumn and winter: pochard, tufted duck, scaup, goldeneye, teal and mallards; gadwall, red-breasted mergansers, pintail, whooper and Bewick's swans occur in smaller numbers. The woods of the park are good in summer for breeding woodcock, blackcaps, spotted flycatchers, treecreepers and long-tailed tits.

• www.eurobirding.co.uk/ireland.htm

3. Fair Head

Sheer basalt cliffs rise almost 200 m from the sea to provide a dramatic coastal landscape. Ireland's last pair of breeding golden eagles nested here in the 1950s. Nowadays, buzzards are common, as are peregrines; sparrowhawks, kestrels, rock doves, ravens and choughs can also be seen.

ARMAGH

4. Lough Neagh: Oxford Island

This part of Lough Neagh provides good viewing facilities, from November to April, for the wintering wildfowl populations. There are several shore-side hides. Goldeneye, pochard, tufted duck, great crested grebes and the other typical Lough Neagh waterfowl can

be seen, together with whooper and Bewick's swans in nearby fields.
- www.eurobirding.co.uk/oxford_island.htm

CAVAN

5. Lough Oughter, east of Killashandra

Best known for holding large numbers of wintering whooper swans. Bewick's swans occur in fewer numbers, while there is a good breeding and wintering population of great crested grebes, little grebes, coots, mallards and tufted duck. In the woodlands there are breeding blackcaps and other interesting woodland species. Not a very well-documented area, and thus offers exciting potential for keen birdwatchers.

DERRY

6. Lough Foyle

Best observation points for the area are at Donnybrewer, Longfield Point, Ballykelly marsh, the Roe Estuary and Magilligan Point. The best time to visit is at high tide, when the waders are pushed close to the shore.

Lough Foyle is the largest sea lough on the north coast. It is shallow and muddy along the southern and eastern sides, and is noted for its large numbers of wildfowl and waders. The best time to visit is late October and early November, when maximum numbers are around. There are large flocks of tundra and whooper swans, brent, white-fronted and greylag geese, pintail, wigeon and mallard to be seen at this time. There are also good numbers of waders: oystercatcher, bar-tailed godwit, curlew, dunlin, lapwing and golden plover; and smaller numbers of greenshanks, redshanks and grey plovers. Great northern, red-throated and, occasionally, black-throated divers are found off Magilligan Point.
- www.eurobirding.co.uk/lough_foyle_rspb_reserve.htm

7. Lough Beg

Lough Beg is one of the best birdwatching areas in the north. It is a shallow lake on the river Bann, flowing north from Lough Neagh to the Foyle estuary. Large numbers of wintering wildfowl are found here: mallard, teal, pochard, wigeon and goldeneye. Whooper and Bewick's swans are winter residents, along with occasional small numbers of greylag geese. The geographical position of Lough Beg funnels many waders into the area during autumn migration – such as greenshanks, black-tailed godwits and common sandpipers, along with many rarities recorded not only in autumn, but also on the return spring migration northwards. There are also good numbers of breeding ducks and waders.

- www.eurobirding.co.uk/lough_beg.htm

8. Roe Valley Country Park, south of Limavady

The park is located along the river Roe and is the best broadleaved, woodland habitat in the region. During the summer, the normal range of Irish, breeding woodland birds can be easily heard and observed, including the sparrowhawk, siskin, chiffchaff, willow warbler and the not-so-common wood warbler.

9. The Bann Estuary

The Bann Estuary is muddy and a good place to watch wildfowl and waders from the security of a National Trust hide. If the hide is locked, collect the key from the nearest of the row of cottages facing the river. The best times to visit are during autumn (September–October) and spring (April–May) migration periods. Common waders such as the redshank, oystercatcher, ringed plover, curlew, knot and dunlin can be seen, along with the shelduck, teal, mallard and wigeon wintering here. The best time of day is during the rising tide.

DONEGAL

10. Inch Lough, south-east of Inch Island, Lough Swilly

A shallow, brackish lough separated from the extensive Lough Swilly by two causeways and Inch Island. Probably the best place in County Donegal for observing wintering and breeding waterfowl. It is the main landfall point in October for Icelandic-bred whooper swans. Wintering birds include greylag and Greenland white-fronted geese, wigeon, teal, shoveler, pintail, pochard, goldeneye, scaup, gadwall and black-tailed godwits. Breeding birds include little and great crested grebes, mallard, tufted duck, coot, sandwich and common terns, dunlin, redshank and black-headed gulls.

11. Sheskinmore Lough, north-west of Ardara

A shallow, sandy lough surrounded by marshland and machair grassland, with sandy dunes nearby. In summer, waders such as dunlin, lapwing, snipe, ringed plover and the common sandpiper breed in the wet meadows and surrounding land. Barnacle and Greenland white-fronted geese are regulars in winter, along with whooper swans, wigeon and teal. Choughs frequently feed on the machair grassland.

12. Horn Head Cliffs

These spectacular cliffs are a major breeding site for seabirds and they also host the largest Irish colony of razorbills. Nesting on the cliffs are guillemots, fulmars and kittiwakes, as well as smaller numbers of puffins, shags, herring gulls, and great black-backed gulls and black guillemots. Ravens, choughs and peregrines are also frequently seen.

13. Glenveagh National Park

A spectacular area in Donegal, with a wide range of habitats –
upland, moorland, oak woodlands, bogland and a large lake,
Lough Veagh. There is an excellent visitor centre as well as
nature trails in the park. Breeding on the uplands are red
grouse, curlews, ring ouzels, peregrines, ravens, whinchats,
wheatears, a few golden plovers and grasshopper warblers.
Breeding on the lakes are one or two pairs of red-throated
divers and some common gulls. The reintroduced golden eagles
are a feature.

- www.eurobirding.co.uk/glenveagh_national_park.htm

14. Malin Head

This rugged peninsula is the most northerly point of Ireland and
an excellent spot to watch offshore movements of seabirds, and
also to observe the arrival of whooper swans, barnacle, greylag and
Greenland white-fronted geese, along with fieldfares and redwings
in September and October. Sea-watching is best during north-
westerly winds, when the birds are pushed close to the headland.

DOWN

15. Copeland Bird Observatory, north of Donaghadee

*Private island. Prior permission should be obtained from the booking
secretary, Neville McKee. Contact: neville.mckee@btinternet.com, or Tel:
028 9443 3068. Boat service from Donaghadee.*

- www.cbo.org.uk

The bird observatory, founded in 1952, is based in the old
lighthouse. Mostly grass-covered, this island is only 16 ha in
size and rises to 30 m on the eastern side. The Manx
shearwater breeding colony of 2,000+ pairs is famous, and the

subject of a long-term (50 years) ringing study. Also breeding are small numbers of fulmars, black guillemots, eiders, red-breasted mergansers, water rails (very easy to see), stock doves, oystercatchers, four species of gulls, etc. The passerine migration is best in spring. The observatory is operated most weekends, and for a few weeks between April and October.

16. Strangford Lough

Strangford Lough is a vast (13,700 ha) sea lough, some 30 km long, with more than 120 islands and extensive mudflats, which cover nearly 50 per cent of the Lough. Large reserves of eelgrass, particularly at the north end, and a rich invertebrate population provide food for a very large number of wildfowl and waders, making this area one of the best bird sites in Ireland. Pale-breasted brent geese occur in big numbers on arrival from arctic Canada in September and October, before dispersing south to other coastal haunts. Feral greylag, barnacle and Canada geese can also be seen, along with big numbers of wintering oystercatchers, knots, redshanks, golden plovers, dunlin and bar-tailed godwits. The islands host breeding duck, tern (up to 700 pairs of sandwich terns) and gull populations. The best time for viewing is September–October, when a vast army of brent geese can be watched foraging through the eelgrass beds.

Visit the Wildfowl and Wetlands Trust Centre at Castle Espie, located on the north-west side of Strangford Lough, 3 miles south of Comber, Co. Down. Open daily. Hides, gift shop, guided walks, etc. Tel: 0289 187 4146.
• wwt.org.uk/visit/castleespie/

17. Dundrum Bay

The inner bay has a representative range of wintering wildfowl and waders. Outside the bay there are common scoters, scaups, goldeneye, long-tailed ducks, divers and grebes. The Murlough Nature Reserve sand dunes are covered by a dense vegetation of sea buckthorn in the south, and heath in the north. Blackcaps, stonechats and grasshopper warblers breed here.

FERMANAGH

18. Lower Lough Erne

This large freshwater lake (22,800 ha) harbours important breeding waterfowl such as common scoters, red-breasted mergansers, great crested grebes and tufted duck, which are concentrated in the Castlecaldwell area. Breeding in the woodlands are garden warblers, crossbills, siskins and redpolls, which are best seen at the RSPB reserve at Castlecaldwell.
• www.eurobirding.co.uk/castlecaldwell_forest_rspb_reserve.HTM

MONOGHAN

19. Dromore Lakes, north of Cootehill

This is a series of 10 small lakes along the river Dromore. During the winter there are good numbers of whooper swans and wigeon, with smaller populations of great crested grebes, herons, goldeneye, lapwings, pochard, tufted duck and mallards.

TYRONE

20. Lough Neagh: West Shore

Lough Neagh is the largest freshwater lake in Ireland, and in Britain too, with a surface area of 383 km². It is of major significance as a wintering area for wildfowl, especially ducks. A representative range of birds – goldeneye, tufted duck, pochard, etc.– can be seen from the pier at Newport Trench and Ardboe Point.

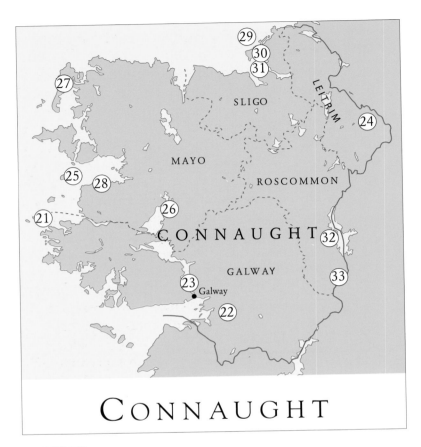

CONNAUGHT

GALWAY

21. Inishbofin Island

Inishbofin is 936 ha in size and is inhabited by about 160 people. Most of the island is rough moorland, with a plantago sward at the west-end. Fulmars, black guillemots, shags and herring gulls breed on the cliffs. Corn buntings and corncakes used to breed. Choughs are a feature. There is a regular boat service from Cleggan, and accommodation is available on the island.

- www.inishbofin.com/index.htm

22. Rahasane Turlough, west of Craughwell

Rahasane Turlough is a low grassy area traversed by the Dunkellin river. During the winter, the turlough fills with water from both underground sources and the river. It is the premier turlough in Ireland, and vast numbers of wildfowl occur here when water levels are low. Wigeon, teal, pintail, shovelers, tufted duck, mallards, whooper and Bewick's swans, as well as Greenland white-fronted geese, will fill the sky when disturbed. It is also a good spot for waders such as golden plovers, lapwings, redshanks, dunlin, black-tailed godwits, and more.

- www.birdwatchgalway.org

23. Lough Corrib

Covering about 17,000 ha, Lough Corrib is the second largest lake in Ireland. Great numbers of pochard and coot, with smaller numbers of tufted duck and goldeneye, congregate in the shallow waters off the marble quarry north of Menlough (on the south-east shore, close to Galway), in October-November. Gadwall and shoveler have been recorded breeding at Mount Ross Inlet, south of Headford, along with great crested and little grebes; tufted ducks, red-breasted mergansers and common scoters breed on some of the islands, along with the gulls, including the common gull and tern.

- www.birdwatchgalway.org

LEITRIM

24. Garadice Lough, east of Ballinamore

A large freshwater lake extending some 360 ha; interesting for breeding great crested and little grebes, mute swans and mallards. In winter, there are whooper swans, wigeon and teal, especially at the west-end. Woodland scrub around the lake host a wide range of passerine species.

MAYO

25. Clare Island

A large inhabited island with about 150 residents. High summit of 400 m and dramatic cliffs along north and western sides. Breeding seabirds include fulmars, guillemots, razorbill, black guillemots and a few puffins. The gannet first bred on the island in 1978, on a low stack to the east of the old tower at the west-end. Good numbers of breeding choughs, peregrines and ravens are frequently seen. There are thriving populations of tree sparrows and "pure" rock doves. Barnacle geese at west-end during April.
• www.anu.ie/clareisland/environment.htm

26. Lough Carra, north of Ballinrobe

A large, shallow, productive lake (1,500 ha) set on limestone and surrounded by reed beds and scrubland. Large breeding population of mallards and tufted duck. Wintering ducks include good numbers of wigeon, teal, shovelers, gadwall, pochard, tufted and goldeneye.

27. The Mullet Peninsula

The Mullet is a long, low, windswept, sandy island separated from the mainland at Belmullet by a navigable channel. Interesting areas to visit include (a) Termoncarragh Lake (whooper swans, Greenland white-fronted and barnacle geese); (b) Annagh Head (seabird and passerine migration); (c) Annagh Marsh and machair grassland (breeding dunlin, redshanks, snipe and lapwings, and formerly the red-necked phalaraope); (d) Cross and Leam Loughs (waders); (e) Blacksod (pale-breasted brent geese,

long-tailed duck and purple sandpipers in the winter).
• www.eurobirding.co.uk/mullet_peninsula.htm

28. Old Head Woodland, north-east of Louisburgh

This is an ancient broadleaved wood dominated by oak, with some alien species. Good range of woodland birds: treecreepers, long-tailed tits, long-eared owls, sparrowhawks. Fulmars nest on nearby cliffs, where choughs and ravens can also be seen cruising. Grey seals offshore.

SLIGO

29. Inishmurray Island

Deserted by the islanders since 1948, this is a low-lying island 6 km from the mainland. There is an important, early monastic site within the cashel. Breeding birds include a thriving population of eiders and storm petrels, with fewer Arctic and common terns, shags and great black-backed gulls. Large numbers of wintering barnacle geese move between this island and the nearby mainland sites at Ballintemple and Lissadell.
• www.rossespoint.com/inishmur.htm

30. Lissadell, west of Carney

The large grass fields alongside the sea at Lissadell are the best mainland site to observe wintering barnacle geese, from October to April. Numbers have increased from 300 to 1,500 in recent years. Mallards, teal, curlew and redshanks also use the freshwater pond in the fields. The geese move between Ballintemple (further west along the coast) and Inishmurray, which explains why they are sometimes absent from Lissadell.

31. Cummin Strand, Sligo Bay

A shallow, sandy bay where large numbers of pale-breasted brent geese and wigeon occur in the autumn and early winter. Large numbers of waders also use the area: lapwings, dunlin, oystercatchers and ringed plovers.

ROSCOMMON

32. Lough Funshinagh, north-west of Athlone

Formerly a famous breeding site for a wide range of wildfowl and rare grebes. There are dense stands of clubrush and reeds at the north-end. Tufted duck, pochard, shovelers, mallards, teal, wigeon, Bewick's and whooper swans, golden plovers, and, occasionally, large numbers of lapwings winter here. Investigation during the summer could be worthwhile.

33. River Shannon: Athlone to Shannon Bridge

The callow lands on either side of the river are attractive feeding habitats to thousands of waterfowl during periods of winter flooding. Greenland white-fronted geese, whooper and Bewick's swans, wigeon, teal, mallards and mute swans, all use the area. Amongst waders, there are large numbers of lapwings, golden plovers and snipe. In summer, the rich grassland pastures are home to the few remaining corncrakes in Ireland.

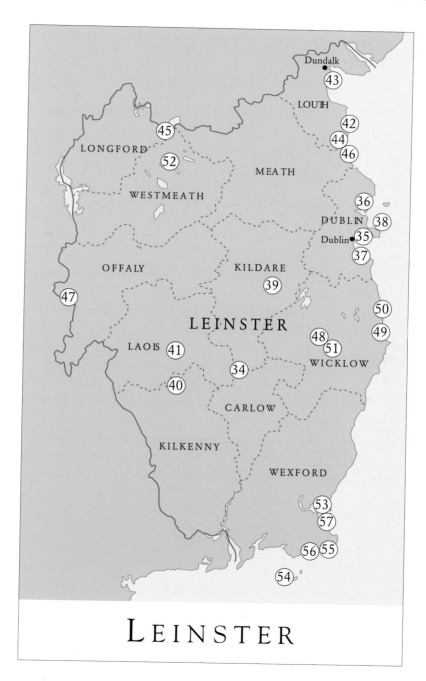

LEINSTER

CARLOW

34. Oak Park Pond, near Carlow Town

This is a small, artificially created lake that, apart from the rivers, is also the only reasonably open water in County Carlow. Mallards, teal and lapwings can be seen, as well as woodland birds in the surrounding trees.

DUBLIN

35. North Bull

The North Bull Island is an extensive sandy island with a sandy beach, sand dunes, salt marshes and a muddy inter-tidal zone between the island and the mainland. It is the best place in Ireland to observe wildfowl and waders because of the birds' tameness, the ease of observation, and the diversity of species here. An interpretive centre on the island has information on the history and wildlife of the place. On the mudflats are pale-breasted brent geese, wigeon, pintail, mallards, teal, shelduck, shovelers and red-breasted mergansers. Large numbers of waders occur: redshanks, knots, dunlin, bar-tailed godwits, oystercatchers, ringed plovers, curlew and turnstones. Irish hares are common on the island.
- www.birdweb.net/bullisland.html

36. Rogerstown Estuary, north of Donabate

The range of species available for viewing is very similar to that at Bull Island. The best time to visit is August to April.

37. South Dublin Bay: Merrion Strand

During the winter, there are brent geese, oystercatchers, sanderling, bar-tailed godwits, ringed plovers and redshanks.

During late July and August, vast numbers of terns return to roost on the strand at dusk, after feeding along the coast, as far south as Kilcoole, Co. Wicklow. Common and Arctic terns are the most numerous, but roseate terns are also present.

38. Ireland's Eye, off Howth

This small island has steep cliffs on its north-east corner, and grassy slopes elsewhere. It is an important seabird-breeding colony, with a recently established (1989) gannet colony, which has about 200 pairs now. Also breeding are fulmars, guillemots, razorbills, kittiwakes, cormorants, shags, black guillemots, a few puffins and the three large seagulls. During the winter, both brent and greylag geese graze the island.
- www.eurobirding.co.uk/irelands_eye.htm

KILDARE

39. Pollardstown Fen, near Newbridge

This fen is of considerable botanical interest. There are good numbers of little grebes, teal, mallards, coot and snipe. Good for water rails.
- www.iol.ie/~nubridge/fen.htm

KILKENNY

40. Ballyragget Creamery Lagoons, south-east of Durrow

These artificial lagoons attract large numbers of golden plovers and lapwings. There are also good numbers of wigeon and teal, along with fewer mallards, pintail, snipe and curlew.

LAOIS

41. Abbeyleix woodlands

These broadleaved woodlands are excellent for a wide and representative range of Irish woodland birds. The estate is private property, and permission to visit should be sought from Abbeyleix House.

LOUTH

42. Clogher Head, north-east of Termonfeckin

A good headland site for watching seabird passage in the Irish Sea, and for monitoring passerine migration. Equally good in autumn (August–October-end) as in spring (March–June), especially after the south-easterly winds, which blow in the migrants from Europe.

43. Dundalk Bay

Dundalk Bay is one of the top European sites for large numbers of waders, particularly oystercatchers, dunlin, knots, redshanks, curlew, bar-tailed godwits, lapwings and golden plovers. Three geese, brent, greylag and Greenland white-fronts sometimes occur, as do many ducks. Visits should be planned to coincide with high tides.

44. Boyne Estuary, Drogheda

Shelducks, mallards, teal, wigeon, black-tailed godwits and other waders are easily seen. Brent geese occur irregularly.

LONGFORD

45. Lough Kinale, near Granard

Lough Kinale is 240 ha in size, with extensive reed beds. Wintering pochard, tufted duck, coot, great crested grebes, whooper swans, wigeon, teal and goldeneye can be seen here.

MEATH

46. Coast off Laytown, south-east of Drogheda

The offshore waters hold great northern and red-throated divers, often a good flock of common scoters, and sometimes scaups.

OFFALY

47. Little Brosna River and Callows

The flooded callow lands attract thousands of duck, mostly wigeon, teal, mallards, pintail and shovelers in the winter. The largest flock of Greenland white-fronted geese outside the Wexford Slobs sojourns here, as do whooper and Bewick's swans. There are also large flocks of waders: dunlin, curlew and black-tailed godwits in particular. The best time to visit is in February and March.

WICKLOW

48. Glendalough Woodlands

The oak woodlands hold a wide diversity of woodland species, including blackcaps, sparrowhawks, the scarce wood warbler and redstarts. Higher above the woods, on the rocky and boggy slopes, ring ouzels can sometimes be seen. Pied flycatchers are a possibility. May and June are the best times for visiting.

49. Broad Lough, north of Wicklow Town

The Lough is long, narrow and tidal, but with a feed of fresh water from the Vartry River. In summer, reed and grasshopper warblers breed in the reeds fringing the northern end, and the rare bearded tit has also been recorded breeding here. Water rails can also be seen without too much difficulty. In winter, the Lough is good for geese (greylags move between here and further north to Kilcoole), swans (whooper and the occasional Bewick's), and ducks (teal, wigeon, mallards and shelducks).

50. Kilcoole Marsh, south of Greystones

This extensive marsh is used by large numbers of greylag and brent geese, as well as Bewick's and whooper swans. There are good numbers of wigeon, mallards and teal, with smaller numbers of shelducks, pintail and gadwalls. Little grebes, curlew, lapwings and redshanks also occur. Breeding on the beach during the summer are little terns and ringed plovers. The area is also good for birds of prey.

51. Glenmalure woods and moorland, south-west of Laragh

The area is one of the best for moorland and upland birds. Siskins, redpolls and crossbills are found in the nearby woods, while ring ouzels, ravens and peregrines can be seen in the more open moorland.

WESTMEATH

52. Lough Derravaragh, south-west of Castlepollard

The Lough is set on limestone and extends over 1,000 ha, with raised bog to the north-west and oak woods on steep banks to the south-east. The lake is an important "staging" site for pochard, mallards, coot and tufted duck. Whooper swans occur, as do smaller numbers of shovelers, pintail and goldeneye.

WEXFORD

53. North Slob, north-east of Wexford Town

Covering about 1,000 ha, this is one of Ireland's premier bird sites. There is a car park, a visitor centre and an excellent observation tower. The slob is famous for the large number of Greenland white-fronted geese. Other geese also occur, particularly brents, which come in from the harbour to feed on the grass fields. Large numbers of Bewick's swans may also be seen, as well as many ducks and wildfowl. The best time to visit is from October to April. The visitor centre has a wildfowl collection, which is indispensable for those who wish to learn how to identify geese and ducks.
• www.eurobirding.co.uk/wexford_slobs.HTM

54. Great Saltee Island

The island is privately owned, but visitors are welcome on day trips. On the island, follow the path up to the throne, and then go south-west to the main gannet colony. Access from the fishing village, Kilmore Quay.

This is the most exciting place in Ireland for intimate views of many different breeding seabirds, such as fulmars, kittiwakes, razorbills, guillemots, shags, gannets, great black-backed herring and lesser black-backed gulls, cormorants and puffins. Choughs, ravens and peregrines are also there, along with many migrating passerine birds during the spring and autumn. May, June and early July are best for the seabirds. Boats depart from Kilmore Quay. Boatman, Declan Bates. Tel: 053 29684.
• www.eurobirding.co.uk/saltee_islands.htm

55. Lady's Island Lake, south of Tagoat

Walk around Lady's Island and enjoy the views over the brackish water. The sandwich, roseate, Arctic and common terns breed on Inish Island (restricted access). Probably the best mainland location in Ireland to see the roseate tern. The great crested and little grebes, mallards, teal, shovelers, tufted duck and Mediterranean gulls have bred here. There are good numbers of wintering wildfowl, as well as many different waders.

56. Tacumshin, south-east of Tomhaggard

The mosaic of vegetation and water in this large 949-ha area provide ideal ecological conditions for a large number of different wildfowl and waders using the area, particularly in September and October. Breeding birds include shelducks, oystercatchers, ringed plovers, redshanks, water rails and many rarities.
• www.eurobirding.co.uk/tacumshin_lake.htm

57. Rosslare Back Strand

This is a good place for waders of Wexford Harbour feeding on mudflats, and roosting along the shore at high tide. Knots, dunlin, oystercatchers, ringed plovers, black-tailed godwits, redshanks, brent geese, wigeon and shelducks are abundant. So are snipe, sometimes forming impressive wisps in the sky. Several tern species can be seen fishing in summer. For wildfowl and waders, visit just as the tide comes in.

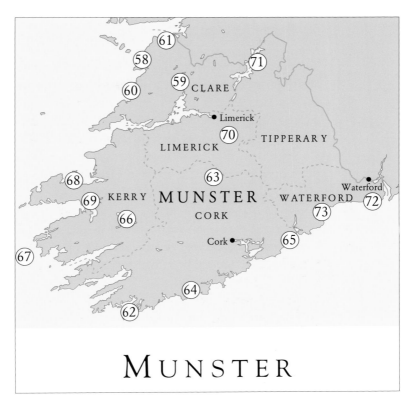

MUNSTER

CLARE

58. Cliffs of Moher

A long stretch of spectacular, horizontally bedded cliffs rising a sheer 200 m from the sea. Excellent views of breeding seabirds: kittiwakes, puffins, razorbills, fulmars, guillemots. Shags, herring and great black-backed gulls also breed. Choughs, ravens, peregrines and rock doves may be seen. Best time is from May to late July. Interpretive centre at cliffs.
- www.eurobirding.co.uk/cliffs_of_moher.htm

59. Ballyallia Lake, north-west of Ennis

This is a rich limestone lake with large numbers of wildfowl, and it also happens to be the most important site for gadwalls in Ireland. Winter birds are whoopers, Bewick's and mute swans, wigeon, teal, pintail, tufted duck, pochard and coot. You will also find curlews, lapwings and black-tailed godwits.

60. Lurga Point, south-west of Quilty

The harbour beach, with its seaweed banks, is the best place in Ireland to see large numbers of purple sandpipers, turnstones, sanderlings and ringed plovers. Offshore is Mutton Island, where several hundred barnacle geese congregate in the winter.

61. Ballyvaghan Bay

Ballyvaghan Bay is a muddy inlet with a shingle spit and several small islands. Good for wildfowl and waders, as well as great northern and red-throated divers. Best location in Ireland to see the scarce black-throated divers. In summer, you will find breeding ringed plovers, oystercatchers, and, sometimes, terns.

CORK

62. Cape Clear Island

This inhabited island is well-known for its rare passerine migrants (best during October) and passing seabirds (best during late July to mid-September). There are nesting razorbills, guillemots and some, although very few, puffins. Choughs, ravens and peregrines breed here. If you want to stay at the Bird Observatory, contact the bookings secretary, Declan Murphy, Birdwatch Ireland,

Rockingham House, Newcastle, Co. Wicklow. Tel: 012819878
- www.eurobirding.co.uk/ireland.htm

63. Kilcolman Marsh, north-west of Doneraile

This is a private sanctuary. Visitors welcome. Please contact Margaret Ridgeway (022-24200) prior to visiting.

This wildfowl refuge area is a limestone-rich marsh that floods in winter. A small number of Greenland white-fronted geese and whooper swans winter here, along with many teal, mallards and wigeon, and fewer gadwalls, shovelers, tufted duck and pochard. Good, close views are available from hides and a special observatory.

64. Clonakilty Bay

Two estuaries comprise Clonakilty Bay, separated by Inchydoney Island. These two muddy bays are good for black-tailed and bar-tailed godwits, oystercatchers, curlews, redshanks, dunlin, grey and ringed plovers, greenshanks and knots. Wigeon winter in the estuaries. Best time to visit is from October to April.
- www.clon.ie/text/system/clewil4.html

65. Ballycotton Bay

Ballycotton Bay is a shallow, sandy bay backed by a complex of lagoons and reed beds at Ballycotton Lake, Shanngarry East and Shanngary West. The area is one of the best sites for seeing ordinary, but also unusual, wading birds during the autumn. In the winter, there is a wide range of wintering wildfowl. Keep to the footpaths, as the fields are privately owned.

KERRY

• www.kerrygems.ie/thingstodo/birds/index.html

66. Killarney National Park

Apart from the common woodland birds, there are jays, blackcaps and long-eared owls. The best places to visit here are the yew woodland at Ross Bay (signposted from Killarney town) and Tomies Wood on the north-west side of Lough Leane.
• www.eurobirding.co.uk/killarney_national_park.htm

67. Great and Little Skellig

These two towering islands are important seabird colonies. Little Skellig has over 20,000 pairs of gannets. Great Skellig has puffins, fulmars, kittiwakes, storm petrels, Manx shearwaters, and more. Boats are available from Portmagee, Cahersiveen and Valentia.

68. Lough Gill, west of Castlegregory

This shallow 1,800-ha lake, mostly fringed by reed beds, is excellent for wintering wildfowl: whooper and Bewick's swans, scaup, mallards, teal, gadwall and shovelers.

69. Castlemaine Harbour

A major brent goose wintering area, with many wildfowl and waders using this vast expanse of muddy, inter-tidal mudflats and associated saltmarshes. Wigeon, pintail, shovelers, mallards and teal can be seen, while in the upper parts of the harbour there are scaup and goldeneye. Best viewing spots are at the south-eastern end of Inch sand spit, Cromane Point and Rossbehy sand dunes on the south side.

LIMERICK

70. Lough Gur, north-east of Holycross

A shallow lake important for wintering wigeon and tufted duck, shovelers, teal, mallards and gadwalls. Whooper and mute swans, coot, cormorants, lapwings and curlew can also be found.

TIPPERARY

71. Lough Avan, west of Borrisokane

Whooper swans, Greenland white-fronted geese and wigeon use the lake for feeding in winter.

WATERFORD

• www.waterfordwildlife.com

72. Tramore Back Strand and Bay

The mudflats are a good place in winter to see a wide range of waders, as well as brent geese. Large numbers of gulls are found at the dump, along with northern wintering gulls (glaucous and Iceland). Best from August to March.

73. Dungarvan Harbour

A similar site to Tramore, with birds easily observed.

WHAT NEXT?

This slim guide provides only the beginning for many people who would like to learn about Irish birds. For those who want to develop this interest, there are several more advanced identification books, which include all the birds that you are likely to see in Ireland. These include:

Collins Field Guide Birds of Britain and Europe by R. Peterson, G. Mountfort and P.A.D. Hollom, published by HarperCollins, 1993.

The Complete Guide to Ireland's Birds by E. Dempsey and M. O'Cleary, published by Gill and Macmillan, 2002.

Birds in Ireland by C. Hutchinson, published by T. and A.D. Poyser, 1989. This is not a guidebook, but a detailed account of all the birds ever recorded in Ireland, with notes on distribution, status and migrations. It is the current standard text on Irish birds.

Ireland's Wetland Wealth by R. Sheppard, published by the Irish Wildbird Conservancy, 1993. A specialist text on wildfowl and waders.

A History of the Birds of Northern Ireland by William M. McDowell. Unpublished CD, 2003. Highly detailed and valuable account of the birds of Northern Ireland.

Seabird Populations of Britain and Ireland by Mitchell, P.I., Newton, S.F., Ratcliffe, N. & Dunn, T.E.(eds.) published by T & A.D. Poyser, 2004. Results from *Seabird 2000* surveys.

Threatened Mammals, Birds, Amphibians and Fish in Ireland by T. Whilde, published by HSMO, Belfast, 1993. An excellent account of all the rare and endangered birds in Ireland.

The New Atlas of Breeding Birds in Britain and Ireland by D. Gibbons, J.B. Reid and R.A. Chapman, published by T. and A.D. Poyser, 1993. An indispensable text on all our breeding birds, with maps.

Atlas of Anatidae Populations in Africa and Western Eurasia by D.A. Scott and P.M. Rose, published by Wetlands International Publications 41.

I-WeBs Report 1998-99 by Kendrew Colhoun. BirdWatch Ireland, Dublin 2001. Extensive report on wildfowl and other wetland birds in Ireland.

The Atlas of Wintering Birds in Britain and Ireland by P. Lack, published by T. and A.D. Poyser, 1986. Another excellent book on all our wintering birds and their distributions.

Ireland: A Natural History by David Cabot, published by HarperCollins, London 1999. New Naturalist No. 84. An extensive account of Ireland's natural history approached from an ecological viewpoint. Standard text on Ireland's natural history.

Wings (Membership magazine of BirdWatch Ireland) No. 29 Summer 2003. Review of rare and scarce breeding birds in Ireland.

There are four major voluntary organisations concerned with Irish birds and their conservation. All provide attractive newsletters, some own and manage bird reserves, organise outings and lectures. Anyone seriously interested in birds should join one or more of these organisations:

BirdWatch Ireland, Rockingham House, Newcastle, Co. Wicklow. Telephone 01-2819878.
• www.birdwatchireland.ie

Northern Ireland Bird Watcher's Association, Wilton Farrelly, Membership Secretary NIBA, 24 Cabin Hill Gardes, Belfast. BT5 7AP

The Royal Society for the Protection of Birds, Belvoir Park Forest, Belfast BT8 4QT. Telephone 0232-491547.
• www.rspb.org.uk/nireland

The National Trust for Northern Ireland, Rowallane House, Saintfield, Ballynahinch, Co. Down. Telephone 0238-510721.
• www.nationaltrust.org.uk

INDEX

The principle reference to each species/group is shown in **bold**